MANAGING PROFESSIONAL
TEACHERS

Biographical details.

Nigel Bennett lectures in educational management in the Centre for Educational Policy and Management of the Open University School of Education. Prior to this he worked at the North East London Polytechnic and before this he taught in secondary education. Along the way he obtained a history degree from Cambridge, an MA in Education from Lancaster, and a PhD in educational management and policy from Brunel. He has worked with teachers from primary, secondary and post-compulsory education on a variety of educational management courses, from introductory to masters' level, and has written for undergraduate and masters' degree courses in the field for the Open University. He has edited two Open University readers, *Managing Change in Education: Individual and Organizational Perspectives* (with Megan Crawford and Colin Riches) and *Improving Educational Management through Research and Consultancy* (with Ron Glatter and Rosalind Levacic), both published by Paul Chapman Publishing.

Managing Professional Teachers

Middle Management in Primary and Secondary Schools

Nigel Bennett
The Open University

P·C·P
Paul Chapman
Publishing Ltd

Names of teachers and schools in this book have been changed.

Copyright © 1995, Nigel Bennett

Paul Chapman Publishing Ltd
144 Liverpool Road
London
N1 1LA

British Library Cataloguing in Publication Data

Bennett, Nigel
Managing Professional Teachers: Middle
Management in Primary and Secondary
Schools
I.Title
371.2

ISBN 1–85396–269–4

Typeset by Whitelaw & Palmer Ltd, Glasgow
Printed and bound by Athenaeum Press, Gateshead, Tyne & Wear

A B C D E F G H   9 8 7 6 5

Contents

Preface

One of the major growth areas of the burgeoning management development field in education has been so-called 'school middle management' training. Most of this training, and of the literature which accompanies it, is narrowly focused on one or both of two limited aims. The first is trouble-shooting: finding immediate solutions to current problems. This often leads to the second: developing an identi-kit manager through the use of checklists of skills and recipes of good practice which can be learned almost by rote and used automatically: here is a meeting, therefore I must do X. Skills-development is obviously important, but an over-emphasis on it at the expense of attending to wider issues can lead to a narrow, mechanistic view of the management role which may be counter-productive if it leads to actions being taken which are inappropriate to the immediate setting. The management adage that it is no use remembering that our objective was to drain the swamp when we are up to our necks in it and surrounded by alligators works the other way too: there is no point in treating your colleagues as if they are alligators if they act more like a herd of deer, and no point in setting alligator traps before draining the swamp if there aren't any there. If we spend all our time rushing around putting right things which are wrong, we may never get round to asking why they are wrong in the first place.

Another growth area has been the development of the concept of reflective practice, which roots itself in immediate problems, but asks the student to think more deeply about the circumstances which give rise to the problem in the first place, often engaging with the assumptions which shape current practice. This, too, is severely practical, but unlike the recipe-book approach it expects the reflective practitioner to look for ideas which may help to generate strategies for dealing with the problem, and to explore the realms of theory as well as others' practice in order to analyse the situation.

Theory can be hard to access, and even more difficult to read and understand. It is also often, and wrongly, seen as the opposite of practice. But theories are only ways of thinking about the world and making sense of it, trying to explain as much as one can in a coherent way. An acceptance of something as good practice derives from reasons for believing it to be good. Theory and practice are indissolubly interconnected. It was, I believe, John Maynard Keynes who stated that those who consider themselves to be the most practical are the slaves to the ghost of some dead scribbler.

This book was born of the wish to provide a source of ideas and reflection for hard-pressed practitioners who wish to improve their understanding of their management role as well as how they perform it. It is hoped that it will inform their problem-analysis and problem-solving, and allow them to go beyond the mere application of recipes and cosy *nostra* from guide books. Its intention is to help teachers who hold, or hope to hold, what are increasingly often called middle management positions to understand more deeply what they have to do as a basis for doing it better. Much management writing which does engage in theory is aimed at senior staff and headteachers: this book attempts to provide material more accessible to staff who have either not yet reached such dizzy heights, or do not wish to.

The book is designed to assist both primary and secondary schoolteachers. It brings together relevant and helpful ideas from the field of general and educational management theory and examines the nature of primary and secondary schools, and the work done within them. It reports on research into management attitudes and expectations in both primary and secondary schools, and concludes with a suggested approach to developing a personal development programme. It makes no claim that primary and secondary schools can be seen through the same set of spectacles: indeed, it questions whether the concept of 'middle management' is necessarily helpful for primary schools.

Along the way, a number of activities have been incorporated into the book, and in some cases I have produced a response which you will find in the Appendix. These activities serve two purposes. Some are designed to try and help you to apply the ideas being explored in that part of the book to your own experience. Others invite you to reflect on your own circumstances to prepare you for the content of what follows. It is hoped that they will encourage you to be more critical about the content and better able to apply what you find helpful to your own situation and personal development.

It should not be thought that I am trying to denigrate the books which offer you approaches to developing what might be called technical management skills. These are important. But there are other abilities which good managers need, and other knowledge which they need to develop, if they are to use the technical skills of management effectively. This book is a practical contribution to that aspect of management development.

I am grateful to many people for their support and assistance during the production of this book. I cannot, of course, name the teachers who were interviewed for the case studies it contains, nor the many heads who returned survey questionnaires, but their contributions were essential. Students on Open University residential schools have argued over some of the ideas and assisted greatly in their development, and colleagues have offered useful critiques.

Some, however, I can name. In particular, I would like to acknowledge the help, support, and encouragement provided by Marianne Lagrange of Paul Chapman Publishing, and Ron Glatter and Sindy York of the Open University's

Centre for Educational Policy and Management. And no writing can be completed without the support of one's family. My thanks to Morag, Alastair and Adrian, who have put up with my absence in the study in the evenings and at weekends, boring conversations, and a serious lack of cricket practice. Without their forbearance, even this work would not have been completed. Its faults, however, are my responsibility alone.

Nigel Bennett

Acknowledgements

The following material is reprinted with permission:

Table 1.1 from S. Whittle and M. Foster (1989) Customer Profiling: Getting into Your Customers' Shoes, *Management Decision*, Vol. 27, no. 6, MCB University Press, p. 28.

Table 3.1 from N. Bennett (1992), E326 Module 1, Unit 1, *Making Sense of Management*, E629 *Managing Educational Change*, The Open University, p. 18.

Table 4.2 from C. Hales (1993) *Managing Through Organization*, Routledge, p. 26.

Table 7.1 from R. J. Campbell and S. R. St. J. Neill (1991) *The Workloads of Secondary School Teachers: a final report*, the Policy Unit, ATL, p. 25.

1

Developing Middle Managers in Schools

Do you ever find yourself complaining about decisions that have been taken in your school? Do you find yourself complaining that it always seems to be your lesson with one particular form that gets disrupted as the school's star football team leaves early for an away fixture? Are you satisfied with the budgetary allowance your department or area of work receives each year, or with the quality of the resources which are available, or with the schedule and arrangements for parental consultations, or the examination timetable? Do you feel entirely happy with the classes you have been allocated for next year? Do you ever find yourself sitting in the staffroom or standing in the playground with a colleague, grumbling about something that has been decided or has taken place, and moaning about 'them'?

If you have to admit to elements of dissatisfaction with your place of work, and have been heard to blame someone else for it, then you have acknowledged that schools, from the smallest primary to the largest secondary, have to be managed. That is, they have to be organised so that the work of teaching and learning can take place, and then kept going so that it can continue. Schools need management.

However, it is only recently that educational management has been acknowledged in the United Kingdom as a legitimate area of study and in-service training, although in the USA it has existed for many years. Some teachers and academics still question whether management has a place in education; others, although accepting that schools and colleges need to be managed, feel that there is little to be learned from writing and practice in commercial and industrial settings. A primary head responded to a survey undertaken in May 1994 as part of the preparation for this book by stating that 'Senior management and middle management are not terms that I find acceptable,' and that he 'did not accept that the term [middle management] was a relevant or appropriate statement'. Despite this continuing resistance to the idea, developments in the United Kingdom since the mid-1970s have created a climate and environment in which educational establishments are increasingly being expected to operate in ways similar to businesses, and teachers have to consider how to respond to these pressures. The pressures which are creating this are outlined in Chapter 2, but first it is appropriate to consider how best to help teachers think about their work and improve on their performance as managers.

THE APPROACH OF THIS BOOK

This book is aimed at helping staff who have responsibility for elements or sections of the work of a school to develop greater skill in carrying out their work. It is hoped that it will also prepare them to take on more senior roles within education. But there are at least two approaches which might be taken towards achieving this aim, which reflect the debate over initial teacher training and the form and content of in-service education and training. One route attempts to define a range of 'management skills' and teach them. In its more sophisticated, 'competency-based' form, it has become the dominant approach to vocational education, and is becoming increasingly common in educational management, where moves have been made to adapt the general management competences identified by the Management Charter Initiative or MCI (see, for example, Earley 1992). Alongside this is a less complex approach, which puts forward some universal basic skills which managers are stated to need. These are often reduced to simple directives or 'how to do it' checklists. For example, in his most recent writings, Jim Donnelly (1994, 1995) has offered checklists for dealing with team-building, supporting weak staff, working with other colleagues, dealing with parents, conducting effective meetings and timetabling. This approach is all very well, and can provide useful ideas and hints to guide practice, but it has major problems. For example, there is a constant emphasis now on team-building, not just in the two articles just mentioned but in works such as Dunham (1995) and Bell (1992). Typically these stress consultation, gaining the involvement of your colleagues in discussion and participative decision-making. It sounds like good advice. But is it always helpful? Consider how useful it is in the following two cases, both of which are drawn from my research. In the first, put yourself in the position of the head of year; in the second, imagine you are the head of one of the two departments.

A suburban girls' school had a policy that every year-group would have an annual day trip which would be entirely separate from the curriculum-related activities normally going on. The head of year seven held a meeting of her form tutors and it was agreed that they would go to a local zoo. This was vetoed by the headteacher. Discussions then took place between the deputy head of the school and the year head, and another proposal was put forward. The tutors didn't like it and said so. At this point the head called the head of year into her study and told her to decide what the children were going to do, and, to use her words, stop 'pussy-footing around'. When the head of year said that she preferred to make decisions 'democratically', the head rounded on her and snapped, 'This school is not run on a democratic basis!'

In another school, there were a number of teachers who taught two or even three subjects, and two departments which had the majority of their classes taught by part-timers. Departmental meetings took place after school in directed time, according to a timetable laid down by the senior management team. The teachers who taught two or more subjects therefore had to resolve split loyalties: which departmental meetings should they attend? How important was it to be 'team members' for a subject in which they taught two classes for one-eighth of their total teaching commitment? What they said they wanted was clear direction and instructions on what was to be done, not lots of time spent in collegial participation in decision-making. The part-time teachers took a similar view: they said that they weren't paid for the time they were expected to spend in meetings, and wished to keep their involvement in the school low and contractual. Team-building and participation wasn't what they chose to do.

The approach to management development through checklists of approved behaviour assumes that certain activities are universally applicable. It also advocates certain approaches to management as being 'right'. For example, a common approach to programmes aimed at teaching good leadership is to use a 'continuum of leadership styles' put forward by Tannenbaum and Schmidt (1973). At one end of the continuum, the leader tells the subordinate what is to be done, and the instruction is carried out. At the other end of the scale, the problem is defined and solved by the workforce and the manager joins in an entirely collaborative and democratic process leading to an agreed decision. It is almost universally agreed in the management training literature that the 'tells' end of the spectrum is bad management. But is it necessarily so? If the school has a set of clearly laid out and defined responsibilities and reporting relationships, and clear rules and procedures, so that it is quite clear who is responsible to whom and for what, then it is entirely appropriate for someone to be 'told' to do something which is within their delegated area of responsibility. The only point at issue is whether you 'tell' them brusquely or 'ask' them politely.

At the other end of the scale is total participation on a consensual or democratic basis in both identifying the problem and making the decision. Much management writing doubts if this is appropriate, and Dunham (1995) quotes with apparent approval an evaluation by teachers of this style as unsatisfactory because it 'totally does away with the manager's input into the decision-making process' (Dunham 1995, p. 23). But why should this be so? Why cannot managers contribute to a decision-making activity on equal terms with their colleagues? Why need 'management' input be separate from 'worker' input? Only if you accept the values that lead to the judgement that they should be.

There is no doubt that we can identify a lot of specific management skills and teach them. But such an approach rests on assumptions that certain types of behaviour are universally desirable in all circumstances and situations. The examples I have given suggest that this may not be so: that the nature of the task, the culture or expectations of the place of work, the nature of the school's structure and organisation and the extent to which it is fluid or rigid, and the legal obligation of those involved as employees, all have a bearing on what is 'right' or appropriate in a particular situation. For that reason, this book takes a second, rather different approach from that of providing over-simple checklists. It will invite you to think about what management involves: what it is supposed to be doing, and how it can be thought about. It will also ask you to relate those ideas to the way your school runs, and to your perception of what it is appropriate to ask of teachers. Hales (1993) has suggested that we should relate what managers do to the way in which their place of work is organised, since organisations are only created in order to facilitate the completion of work. In other words, I shall ask you to take an analytical and reflective approach to considering what your work involves you in doing, so that you can identify the particular management skills which you need to develop. In the course of this book, therefore, we shall examine the following questions:

- What do we mean by 'management'?
- What is meant by 'middle management'?
- What is meant by 'school middle management', and is this the same for primary and secondary schools?
- What constrains and influences management activity and practice?
- How can managers exercise the functions of management?
- What do managers need to learn?

However, before embarking on this activity you must decide whether you are prepared to accept that education and management can be related to one another, or whether you accept the view of the primary head who was quoted earlier. The rest of this chapter will examine the claim that education is unique, and therefore should not attempt to import ideas from general management theory and training.

Activity 1
What is your response to this claim? Is education 'unique'? Jot down your answer before reading on.

MANAGEMENT AND EDUCATION

The case against applying management thinking to educational settings rests on two basic premises. The first, which addresses issues of educational goals and purposes, is that it reduces the work of education to mere technical concerns, instead of engaging with important moral questions of what should be done. The second, which is concerned with both purpose and process, argues that education is a unique activity which cannot be analysed except in its own terms. Bottery (1992), for example, claims that thinking in terms of managing education diverts attention from the need to generate an ethical basis for all action within educational establishments. He acknowledges that there are insights to be found in management literature, but argues that they

cannot be applied directly or uncritically to school
before they are any use. He has also been unhapp
managers, claiming that 'effective management' is sim
own way in the quickest, most convenient manner' (L
Winston (1992) also outlines two of the arguments put
and 1980s: that management thinking turns the business
from a practical into a technical activity, thus making us thin
of achieving some known end or purpose, instead of consid
when faced with competing and possibly conflicting moral idea
and that it focuses entirely upon what is achievable rather
acceptable, pushing moral questions to the margins of educational discussion
(Fielding 1984; Bottery 1988).

There is certainly a danger that if we take a narrow and mechanistic view of
management, focusing on 'tips' and techniques for particular activities, we can
lose sight of the purposes behind the actions. It is precisely because of this
concern that some management writers are inviting managers, in business and
commerce no less than in education and the public sector, to revisit their
assumptions about why they do what they do, as well as trying to do it better.
Management, as Shipman (1990) and Glatter (1988), among others, have
pointed out, is not an end in itself, but a means to particular ends. It can be
presented as concerned with what Carr (1987) wishes to define as 'technical'
issues – with achieving defined objectives rather than with the generation of
goals and values. However, the view of management which Shipman and
Glatter offer emphasises that the values which have defined the goals being
pursued must also underpin the means taken towards their achievement, both
by those doing the managing and by those being managed. Otherwise the
means adopted towards the ends could actually prevent the achievement of
those ends. As Day, Whitaker and Johnston (1990) argue, managers must be
judged on the outcomes of their work, not on their plans and policies. This is
true whether they are managers of a factory, a school or a social work
department. Thus management action must always rest upon a set of values:
what is right and good behaviour, and what can best achieve the goals which
are set or agreed.

This is not to say that the ends can always justify the means: quite the
reverse. It is possible for secondary schools to inflate their A-level points score
in the annual 'league tables' by only entering for the examination the children
who are certain to get high grades, but this may not be the way to improve the
overall standard of academic performance of the sixth form. Managers, in
school or factory, have to recognise that a key influence on those whom they
manage is how they and other managerial colleagues behave, just as a key
influence on children's behaviour is not what their teachers tell them to do, but
what they actually do themselves. Teachers who push to the front of the queue
at lunchtime cannot expect their children to wait in an orderly line; managers
who take very large pay rises cannot expect their employees to accept small
increases.

break away from the view of management as simply a set of ...es to be applied in the correct way in a given setting, we acknowledge ... management is fundamentally value-driven. This implies that the adaptation required by Bottery is one of seeking to match proposed practice with the underlying values of the school. At this point we run up against the second of the arguments against applying management thinking to educational settings: that education is a unique activity, and that the values which are embodied in educational activity are incompatible with those which underpin the writings of management theorists.

IS EDUCATION 'UNIQUE'?

There is no doubt, as philosophers since Plato have demonstrated, that educational activity must take into consideration what are acceptable purposes for it to seek to fulfil. The problems arise when we try to identify who has a legitimate stake in defining what is acceptable, and what procedures and methods are legitimate in attempting to reach that definition. Education is, for most teachers and pupils, a public undertaking. It rests on public funding, and clear legal and moral obligations result from that status. It is arguable that those who are specialists in the work of teaching should be involved in defining acceptable goals and strategies for their achievement. But it is also arguable that the public agencies which take decisions on the levels of spending on education should also be involved in deciding what that money should be used for. Further, they can claim to define the participants in such a debate, including, should they wish, parents or other 'consumers'. There is, then, a debate to be held between the public's decision-makers and the specialists on what is acceptable and feasible, and what should be done to try and achieve the goals decided. Whilst the specialists can argue for moral and ethical questions to be taken into consideration, other participants in the debate can also argue for different codes of ethics to be considered. This suggests that questions of value-for-money and efficiency are legitimately part of the discussion which must surround both goals and means in education.

Two particular problems are created by the debate between public funders and educators: how to provide both for large numbers of pupils and for individuals, and how to judge success. In addition, because teachers are dealing with individuals they need to have considerable freedom of action or 'discretion' (Lipsky 1980) in deciding what to do, when and how. These three considerations are sometimes the basis for claiming that education is a unique activity. However, other aspects of social activity have similar problems and have to come to terms with the imperatives created by their being publicly funded, notably social work and medical practice. Lipsky (1980) examined the consequences for social work and education of their being branches of public policy, and argued that both social workers and teachers deal with the problems in similar ways: they categorise their clients (children, in the case of teachers) into groups whom they can then 'batch process' for their work. The social workers he studied frequently categorised cases into straightforward and complex, and worked on the complex cases for the first part of the week, before clearing their desk of the straightforward problems in the later part of the week: that way, they appeared to be efficient, but the consequence was that cases were sometimes dealt with in a summary way when they needed more detailed and careful handling. In schools, children are organised into classes, and sometimes grouped by ability, especially at secondary level. Classes and children develop reputations, often informally within the staff: classes get described as easy or difficult, and individual children become categorised, in order to generate appropriate strategies for dealing with them and to make particular practices acceptable. It is legitimate to take certain forms of action towards difficult classes, low-ability groups, or individuals with particular problems which might not be acceptable with good classes, top band groups, or naughty children. The process is similar for both teachers and social workers.

The problem of measuring success or achievement is similar. Under the terms of the Education (Schools) Act 1992 and its attendant Circulars, schools have to publish examination results and other measures of achievement such as truancy rates in particular ways, but attempts to amend these results or add 'glosses' to them which allow particular emphases to be placed on what they are doing, led to successive attempts to tighten up the regulations. By 1994 it was no longer possible for schools to 'massage' the GCSE results by not entering the least able children, but they can still inflate their A-level scores in this way. The problem of measuring success in school is nothing new, and is not unique to teachers: when I was at secondary school I belonged to the school house which always came bottom in the sports competition for 'cock house', much to the shame of our housemaster, a great sporting buff. A succession of house captains, however, placed great emphasis in their termly 'reports' to the house meeting on the large number of clubs and societies which house members ran, which far outstripped the contributions of the other three houses. Nor is it unique to education, as the reference to Lipsky shows: the social workers he studied manipulated their efficiency figures to complete a steady throughput of cases. In another study of public policy in action, Rein (1983) demonstrated how an individual social worker could convert a case wherein the client had decided she was getting nowhere and chose therefore to opt out of counselling into a successfully concluded case.

The issue of discretion is clearly addressed in the previous examples. Indeed, it has been more extensively examined in the field of social welfare policy than in education. Social workers and doctors need to have the freedom to decide what action is appropriate in a given setting, just as teachers do: indeed, it is arguably more important for doctors than for teachers!

These examples suggest that education may not be as unique as is sometimes claimed. However, workers in these other areas of public policy have also questioned whether general management principles can be applied to their areas of work. It is certainly the case that the same kind of debate over the values which underpin the actions of the people delivering the service and their relation to those who are accountable for its delivery to the funding agencies is visible in medicine, social work and education. Perhaps the issue is not that education is unique, but that public services are different from industry and commerce, and so the principles of management for those services are different.

Keep (1992) has pointed out that the basis of funding public services is different from the sources of income for private enterprises and creates restrictions and constraints which make it difficult to transfer assumptions automatically from the private to the public sectors. However, if we acknowledge that the values which underpin the goals and practice must also inform management practice, then the issue becomes how one applies, or judges the applicability of, management precepts from one sector to another, or from one setting to another.

It is a great mistake to see private enterprise management as in some way uniform and monolithic. It is quite likely that some readers will be thinking by now that the argument that education can be analysed as a public service has understated unique aspects of each of the public services drawn upon. The same point could be made about education itself. Primary schools and secondary schools are different, perhaps fundamentally so. Large schools are different from small schools, rural schools (especially small rural schools) from urban schools, multi-ethnic schools from ethnically homogeneous schools, grammar schools from comprehensive schools, single sex schools from mixed schools, and so on. The degree of difference between the various categories varies, and certain key features are common to all of them, but in most cases there are basic differences in assumptions and values. Similar kinds of differences can be identified in many private sector organisations: not only do they vary in size from a few staff to hundreds of thousands, and from one small site to many large factories, but there are other differences too: some are concerned with production, and others with the delivery of services; some are operating with a profit in mind, while others enjoy charitable status and may not make a profit; some are concerned to deliver large numbers of identical products, while others are concerned to customise their output. Sometimes what the companies produce can be so different that the patterns of management control which are needed are radically different: for example, Keep (1992) comments that the management needs and processes for a fast food outlet are likely to be substantially different from those of a computer software house. The nature of what is called the 'primary task' – what the managers are supposed to be making sure is completed successfully – is a major consideration when one considers what represents appropriate management activity in the private sector. Whittle and Foster (1989) identified a number of differences between 'products' and 'services' which might be the outputs of commercial organisations (see Table 1.1). It would be helpful for you to consider how many of the characteristics that they attribute to commercial services could also be applied to schools.

Table 1.1   The difference between products and services

Products	Services
Tangible	Intangible
Uniform	Non-uniform
Consumption follows production	Production and consumption occur simultaneously
Non-perishable	Perishable
Production is buffered from customers	Customers participate in the service, sometimes as 'partial employees'
Under management and supervisory control	Often delivered away from managerial and supervisory control
Customer requirements can usually be stated and measured unambiguously	Customer requirements evasive, difficult to identify
Technology dominated	People dominated

Source: Whittle and Foster 1989, p. 28.

Many of these characteristics of 'services' seem to me to apply without much difficulty to the work of schools, and suggest that the 'education is unique' argument does not hold. Bottery (1994) may be coming to a similar conclusion. He cites with approval Leat's (1993) suggestion that organisational types may be more important than sector differences. She points out that, for example, there is much in common between running Oxfam and ICI, because they are large, do many things, and operate in many places throughout the world. Similarly, there may be much in common between the tasks involved in running a market stall and running a playgroup in the local church hall: they are small, have a relatively limited number of clients, and provide a clearly defined service. ICI and the market stall have little in common for their management, but are 'private sector commercial', while Oxfam and the playgroup are profoundly different management concerns but are non-profit-making charities. Does the idea of 'sectors' provide much guidance in analysing management issues in these cases?

Just as management in business and commerce contains within it a wide variety of needs and practices, so general management theory is neither monolithic nor universal. Like all theory, it contains a variety of schools of thought and a wide range of propositions of good practice. Much of it is normative rather than analytical: that is, it seeks to generate universal 'oughts' rather than critical discussion. However, it is possible to use it analytically and critically, examining the assumptions behind the writing and treating it as a heuristic, to be tested and adopted as and when it seems to be useful. That is what this book tries to do.

The point at issue is that education should not regard itself as unique or monolithic, nor should it see management theory as monolithic. Bottery's (1992) attack on management theory as needing application, not uncritical acceptance by teachers, is true of all management theory in relation to all organisations. What is necessary is to consider the assumptions which underpin the view of the management task and the ways in which that task should be carried out. Management is a process geared to the achievement of particular purposes in particular settings, and should be influenced by those purposes and settings.

It is therefore reasonable to approach the management elements of teachers' work through a managerial analysis. That will be started in Chapter 3, when we will discuss a variety of ways of looking at what managers do, and how the work of 'middle managers' is influenced by the structure and culture of the organisation in which they work. But schools are not isolated from the world in which they operate, and they have to take account of a range of external pressures. Those pressures have created the climate in which management has become a major focus of in-service training, and have a strong bearing on the nature of the so-called 'middle management' role in schools. Chapter 2 outlines these pressures and expectations, and begins to develop a view of the managerial needs of the schools' response.

2

Why Schools May Need
'Middle Managers'

Thirty years ago there were no courses of advanced study in educational administration or educational management in the United Kingdom. Now there are plenty to choose from: a recent study by Lawrence (1994) identified sixty-one Masters' degree programmes in England and Wales which included substantial elements of educational management study. As well as MA and MEd qualifications, there are now several MBA (Master of Business Administration) courses specialising in educational management. What has provoked this upsurge in qualifications in a field which a few years ago hardly existed? The answer lies in the policy background created by the British government since 1979.

THE POLICY BACKGROUND

The pressures on schools which have given rise to this interest in management training and development have been created by central government's determination since 1979 to make public services, wherever possible, subject to the same pressures and 'disciplines' which are created for private companies by their need to sell their products in a market. This policy rests on the belief that the fundamental requirements of market economics – freedom for the customer or client to choose between a variety of potential suppliers, and the need to ensure that those suppliers are genuinely competing for the customer's interest – are the most efficient way of ensuring that quality services are provided by government agencies at minimum cost. Thus local government must put many of its services out to tender, and its own employees have to bid for the contract to deliver those services in competition with private companies. Government then becomes the means of regulating the standards of service and monitoring the quality of what is provided, rather than providing them directly.

The word 'efficient' is important here, for it points to another major aspect of government thinking which has implications for schools. Governments must always pay attention to how public money is spent, and must require from the people who are authorised to spend it a suitable account of what they do. The 1980s saw a higher profile given to the work of government auditors, which led to the National Audit Office being created as an agency independent of any government department. Since the present government has operated throughout its life on the rhetoric of reducing public spending and the tax burden on its citizens, its need to stress the importance of financial accountability creates a tension in its policies between freeing the public sector so that it can operate in the market and controlling its actions to ensure that public money is properly used. Consequently, as freedom to act has apparently been devolved to the agents delivering the services, the regulatory mechanisms controlling their actions, and the specifications of what those services are to provide, have been tightened.

In education, this has been visible in a number of ways. We must draw a distinction between developments in England and Wales and those in Scotland, which has its own educational system, so that the starting-point for reform is different, and where it has been more difficult for the government's ideas to become widely accepted. South of the border, the specification of what should be provided by schools has increasingly been tightened, first through the requirement that all LEAs were to frame and implement policies on the school curriculum (DES circulars 6/81 and 8/83), and then through the provision of money for the Technical and Vocational Education Initiative (TVEI) and its attendant in-service training. Schools' capacity to provide the required curriculum was influenced through several revisions to the arrangements for funding in-service training, which also reduced the freedom of action which local authorities had to provide other forms of training. Alongside this came a sustained professional debate orchestrated by HM Inspectorate. This was clearly a move to impose accountability pressures on the local authorities, and ran alongside wider attempts to curb local government spending through such moves as revisions to the ways in which local government grants were calculated, the introduction of rate-capping and the reform of local government funding through the introduction of poll tax and its successor, the council tax. All of these measures can be seen as deriving from the drive for closer financial accountability: the wish to see improved services in return for financial grants.

The second half of the 1980s saw a change of central government's attitude towards local government in general which had consequences for education. Whereas the first thrust had been to try and make local authorities more efficient through stronger financial controls, the second thrust attempted to alter the way in which they delivered their services. At this point the idea of the market became the dominant theme. Local authorities were to become contracting agents, buying from private organisations the services they had to provide, monitoring their provision and applying quality control and assurance inspections as necessary. However, there were some problems in applying this across the board. In particular, education and social services provided specialist work for which the private sector was ill-equipped, although there was already considerable private provision in certain areas, such as residential nursing care for the elderly and, of course, independent schools.

The solution adopted was to strengthen further the central regulation of the system which had begun with the demand for LEA curriculum policies, but to create a quasi-market in which schools could be made largely independent of local authority control and direction. A national curriculum was prescribed by the Department of Education and Science (as it was then called). State schools received a grant based on the number and needs of the pupils they provided for, and were given considerable freedom thereafter in how they spent it. Responsibilities were given to school governing bodies to make expenditure decisions, so creating some 'consumer involvement' in determining what schools did. The freedom given to parents to choose their children's schools was theoretically increased, in the belief that the quality of what schools did in delivering the national curriculum would have a bearing on their popularity and therefore on the grant they received. Local authorities became the agents through which money was disbursed to schools, and the providers of support services for the teachers and others involved. Thus parental choice, resting on the quality of provision, was to be the market force which would determine the level of funding of the individual school. Good schools would be allowed to expand up to a predetermined size, whereas failing schools would have to turn their efforts around or close. The LEA was to be marginalised into the quality control agent.

Since then, developments have moved the public education service further towards a market system. Government enthusiasm for Grant Maintained Schools, free of local authority control, have led to the creation of the Funding Agency for Schools and its Welsh equivalent, independent of the LEAs. Local authority advisory and support services are increasingly becoming self-funding agencies, contracting with schools to provide assistance and competing with private consultants. Grant Maintained schools were permitted to apply to become specialist schools in particular curriculum areas, thus increasing the diversity of choice available to parents, and all schools can now apply to become 'technology colleges' if they can obtain private funding. In all these ways, schools in England and Wales are increasingly being seen as operating in a market, buying the services they require from specialist agencies, competing with other schools for the patronage of parents, and selling their services to those parents in return for money which is paid on behalf of the parents by the funding agency or LEA.

Although the situation in Scotland has not changed as far as it has in England and Wales, considerable attempts have been made there, too, to increase the extent to which the education system is influenced by the market. There was always more central regulation of the curriculum in Scotland than in the rest of Great Britain, but considerable moves were made to introduce forms of parental choice ahead of those which developed in England and Wales. Further, the Scottish Office Education Department has developed a range of projects for reviewing school performance which have incorporated parents into the evaluative process. However, Scottish school boards have less autonomy from the LEA than governing bodies in England and Wales, financial delegation to schools has not moved anywhere near as far, and moves to introduce grant maintained schools in Scotland have proved an almost total failure.

Whichever part of the United Kingdom your school is in, it is not operating in an entirely free market. The schools which receive public money have to deliver the national curriculum, carry out the tests and assessments laid down by statutory orders, and publish their achievements in approved ways. Even though attempts have been made to reduce the extent to which the national curriculum constrains what schools do, it remains a major limitation on their freedom of action. Although schools are free to exclude children once proper procedures have been followed, it is to be made difficult for them to refuse access to children unless they are already full, so as to preserve the rights to education of children with statements of special educational need. This is encouraging schools to create situations in which they are not simply full but oversubscribed, since a waiting list can be used as an excuse for not accepting unwanted children from elsewhere. LEAs and funding councils will have responsibility for securing adequate educational provision, and also for ensuring that surplus places are taken out of use. Over-provision is not to be an option: it is, therefore, to a considerable extent a rigged market.

The changes which have been sketched briefly here have changed quite fundamentally the tasks which have to be discharged in schools. Teaching by teachers in order to promote learning by pupils remains at the centre of the work of a school, but the nature of that teaching and learning, and the tasks which surround it, are different in nature and seriously extended in range and scope compared to the late 1970s. In designing courses and planning lessons, teachers have to take account of the requirements of the national curriculum and key stage assessments. Central government regulations are requiring schools to undertake annual planning activities to consider how they bring in new curriculum requirements, and how they provide staff development and other activities to ensure that the teachers are fully equipped to teach them. With the delegation to schools of financial responsibilities, a range of planning and control activities have to be carried out, covering not just traditional 'capitation' expenditure on books and equipment but also a range of staffing and premises costs formerly borne by the local authority. As a result of the increased emphasis on accountability, schools are now required to appraise their staffs. Governors, too, are supposed to provide a lay input to professional activities and to monitor what is happening, thus requiring forms of reporting which were not previously needed.

Alongside the structural changes outlined above, the education service has also experienced a range of professional changes over the same period. The 16+ examination structure in England and Wales was altered in 1989 to provide a common examination for all pupils: GCSE replaced GCE O-level and CSE. The TVEI scheme was extended to cover all schools. Attempts were made to reform the 18+ examinations, but these foundered on political opposition; however, an additional academic sixth form examination, the AS-level, was introduced. Similar attempts have been made north of the border to reform the 'O' Grade (now Standard Grade) and 'Highers'. Schools came under increasing pressure to develop a stronger vocational focus for their work. TVEI was a part of this, but there was also a broader thrust to have schools introduce BTEC programmes and City and Guilds awards and to move towards competency-based qualifications – National Vocational Qualifications (NVQs) and broader General NVQs. Schools were asked to consider profiling schemes for recording pupils' achievements, and also required to introduce appraisal. All these changes in the field of professional practice have implications for those who are responsible for schools.

RESPONDING TO A NEW POLICY CLIMATE

It is clear from this thumb-nail sketch that the change experienced by the public education service has been wide-ranging and rapid. It was widely recognised that teachers and others working in schools needed assistance to weather the changes and continue to deliver their primary responsibility of educating children. In this context of widening imposed change and an increasingly competitive environment, some writers and teachers have turned to the worlds of business and commerce, in which competition and change are the norm. Do they have anything to teach us about the process of coping with change and responding to it successfully?

Keep (1992) points out that there are some crucial differences between the public and private sectors of the economy which may reduce the extent to which models can be transferred from one to the other. He lists the following ways in which the public sector is different:

- It is more susceptible to political interference.
- It is unable to price its services in the same way as the private sector; instead, it is expected to provide a service for a fee which is set in advance according to a formula defined elsewhere. It cannot therefore think in terms of making a profit.
- It has very limited discretion over what it can provide and how it can spend the money it receives: it cannot go in for deficit budgeting, realise its assets by selling off redundant ground or buildings, raise capital through loans or 'rights issues', or change drastically its 'product mix' to take account of perceived changes in market wishes.

These points are important when we start to consider in detail how staff in schools can respond to the changes they face. They are increasingly recognised in the political arena, and at the time of writing (early 1995) ideas such as allowing colleges and universities to borrow against their property assets to fund capital projects suggest that some of the restrictions which prevent the public sector operating fully on market principles may soon be eased. Even if these restrictions remain, however, it does not follow that there is nothing to be learned from the business and commercial world. It is, for example, a characteristic of competitive environments that the organisations within them seek to differentiate themselves from each other, whence the importance of brand names and advertising identities. But the work of differentiating one's company and its products or image from its competitors also carries as its reverse side the need to ensure that its products and activities are consistent. Maverick producers or executives are unlikely to be tolerated unless the image which the company wishes to promote is one of individuals pursuing their own ideas and following their own initiatives. This is also true of education. A primary school which presents itself to parents and prospective parents as a traditional school which stresses the learning of basic skills is unlikely to tolerate for long a teacher who employs non-traditional methods. One of the central propositions of much management writing in the 1980s has been that in coping with rapid and substantial change it is important to develop a consistent response which is widely accepted among the staff. In achieving this, it is widely acknowledged in management studies that the key factor needed in any organisation is leadership.

Activity 2.1

Before going on, you might like to consider these three questions.

• What does leadership involve?
• Who exercises leadership in your school?
• How successful and effective is the leadership that is provided?

I can't answer the last one, of course, but the next section examines the first two.

LEADERSHIP AND MANAGEMENT

Leadership has been conceived of in a number of different ways since it was first the subject of systematic social investigation. Bryman (1992) identifies the school of thought which has developed in the 1980s as the 'new leadership' school. 'New leadership' writers see the central task of leaders as being to create and communicate a *vision* of what is wanted. Bryman comments that vision is in danger of becoming an overworked term, a panacea of management consultants, but acknowledges that it is, nevertheless, a crucial element of leadership. By vision the writers of the 'new leadership' school mean a perception of the basic values which the leader wants to inform all the actions undertaken in the organisation: a picture of the ideal future. The leader should communicate this vision and its associated values through everything that she or he does. Leadership gives direction to the work of others, helping them to see what is wanted in a particular setting, and how it should be achieved. It shapes the assumptions about what is proper and good behaviour, and so works to create the norms which underpin the day-to-day actions of the people who work in the organisation or unit. In this work of developing and communicating norms, expectations and values to their colleagues, leaders provide a stable element in an unstable environment. They also work to interpret that environment on behalf of their colleagues and make sense of the demands it is making on the organisation and the people who work in it.

You will no doubt have realised that there is an assumption in all this that leadership needs to be exercised *over* and *on behalf of* the people doing the job. This separation of 'leadership' from 'work' on the core activity – producing cars, providing a service to customers, or teaching children – is a fundamental assumption about the needs of almost all organizations except for very small ones.

An important aspect of this leadership function is that those who exercise it share their vision of the organisation and its attendant values with those whom they lead, and try to inculcate the same values and vision into their colleagues. This is a significant activity in a time of rapid change, for although it does not remove from individuals the responsibility of coming to terms with the demands of the changes and their impact on practice, it provides assistance and possibly direction to their efforts. Strong leadership and 'weak followership' may lead to uncritical acceptance of the interpretation put forward by the leader; 'strong followership', in which the ideas of the leader are scrutinised critically and debated, may produce some negotiation, but the eventual interpretation of what is needed will probably be stronger.

This view of the centrality of leadership, although a key dimension of current management literature, is in reality nothing new, and has, indeed, a long tradition in educational history and thought, where we can read about great figures of nineteenth-century education such as Thomas Arnold of Rugby and Edward Thring of Uppingham. The picture of the headteacher as crucial leader of the educational enterprise is a powerful image in much educational writing, and there is a considerable amount of evidence to suggest that teachers do indeed look to the headteacher for leadership. Bolam *et al.* (1992), for instance, cite evidence from primary school teachers that good headteachers set the directions in which the school is to go, and are forceful and decisive. Much earlier, Nias (1980) identified three styles of leadership exerted by primary heads – autocratic, participative and 'Bourbon' – and found that what staff asked for was consistent and positive leadership. Whether they would accept Thring's statement (in Jennings 1977) that 'I am supreme here and I brook no interference' is another matter, although this attitude may be more common than might be acknowledged!

Writing which rests on exhortation rather than evidence similarly places the headteacher/leader at the centre of the educational enterprise: the 1992 White Paper *Choice and Diversity* (DFE 1992) writes (para. 1.33) of 'teachers of high quality under the strong leadership of the headteacher', while Alexander, Rose and Woodhead (1992) in what became known as the 'Three Wise Men' report, identified five key leadership functions of primary school headteachers: quality assessment and assurance, monitoring teachers' work, working alongside teachers, vision, and delegating work to curriculum co-ordinators.

There is, therefore, considerable congruence between what is seen as the hallmark of an effective *managerial* response to uncertain and turbulent environments and an effective *educational* response to rapid change. However, leadership must of necessity take the broad view. The leader within the school must create a vision which integrates the many changes and the responses which individuals and groups should make into a coherent whole. Change, however, is a difficult and messy activity. As McLaughlin (1990) comments, the problems of implementing changes always occur at the smallest unit within the organisation. Curriculum changes ultimately depend on individual teachers working in individual classrooms. Further, change is not a sequence of events, but both a sequence and a series of parallel activities, all taking place at once in a variety of settings and circumstances (van der Vegt and Knip 1990). They argue that innovation involves the creation of both 'structural linkages' between those involved, which can carry information and make necessary physical and organisational arrangements, and what they call 'normative linkages', which allow those involved to share and develop common expectations about the ideals behind the innovation and appropriate behaviour towards their achievement. For example, national curriculum Science was implemented in every school science department in a range of different classrooms and laboratories by a number of different teachers – simultaneously. The extent to which it was successfully introduced can be argued to depend on satisfactory arrangements for equipment and resources, appropriate timetabling arrangements, and agreement on how to turn the new syllabuses and guidelines into practice. So while leaders may shape the ways in which it is *decided* to put the innovation into practice, they cannot hope to follow through on all the different activities involved once the decision moves into *action*. They need assistants who can transmit the vision on through the organisation, articulate it in practical terms, and work with their colleagues to turn it into reality. This is a key role for that group commonly referred to as 'middle managers'.

The concept of 'middle management', then, carries with it an important view of their obligation to their colleagues, and the source of that obligation. Like the concept of leadership, it implies separating responsibility for channelling the response and disseminating the values of leaders from the business of carrying out the core task. It assumes a downward flow of authority from the leader of the organisation, given in order to promote what the leader seeks. To conceive of staff as operating in 'middle management' roles is to locate them in an essentially hierarchical view of the organisation. They become the faithful dischargers of instructions. Although the idea of schools as hierarchies is widely disliked – indeed, it may have been this, rather than the idea of 'management', that so upset the primary head quoted in Chapter 1 – this view is in fact widely accepted in practice. Bolam *et al.* (1992), for example, continued their summary of desired characteristics of good leadership by indicating that once the head had set the direction of policy, teachers wanted to have responsibility for achieving the goals handed over to them. It is important to note the idea of responsibility being 'handed over', for this implies clearly that it originates in the headteacher/leader and is delegated to the staff. This is in line with the formal accountability of the headteacher to the school's governors for everything which goes on in the school. Middle management, then, is concerned with spreading the vision and delivering it in practice in the wide range of classroom and other activities which make up the daily work of schools.

However, it would be wrong to create the idea that middle managers in school are concerned only with passing ideas and information down the line from leader to followers. The leaders of any organisation need to be kept informed of what is going on in the daily work, and where problems are arising. The people who are trying to sustain and realise the vision are also an important source of information on problems and opportunities. Thus Earley and Fletcher-Campbell (1989) found that headteachers and advisers saw a major characteristic of the 'good' head of department that they could take a whole-school perspective on their work, and did not limit their thinking to the narrow confines of their subject area. The wider picture would allow them to inform their seniors of problems for the school as a whole.

Activity 2.2
How do you react to the idea that your head of department – or, if that is what you are, you personally – should act primarily as the agent of the head and senior staff? You might care to return to this question at the end of the book! I comment on my personal reaction to this question in the appendix.

Unfortunately, the idea of the middle manager as the representative of senior management to the staff in what Becher and Kogan (1980) christened the 'basic units' which deliver the school's teaching (departments, subject areas, curriculum teams, pastoral houses or years, etc.) does not sit comfortably with the view of teaching as a professional activity. This places the source of a teacher's authority not in the post held but in the training and experience which each individual possesses. The view of teaching as a professional activity sees it as something difficult which cannot be routinised: as one head of department said in interview, 'I want teachers in my department, not robots.' Teaching involves dealing constantly with a range of problems, deciding what to do about them and correcting or adapting plans accordingly. An example might be having to abandon the planned lesson because heavy snow has resulted in half the class being absent; the teacher doesn't start a new topic but invents something for the children to do instead. More common would be having to adapt one's teaching strategy in order to help a small group of children who were struggling to grasp a basic idea, while allowing the rest to practise what they appeared to have mastered. Such a realistic view of teaching is often extended to the claim that teachers cannot, therefore, be expected to 'deliver' an externally generated or imposed curriculum: they must have discretion (Lipsky 1980, Young 1981) to decide what and how to teach. Their obligation is to their professional commitment to doing the best for their children, rather than to 'the management'.

As we have seen, this tension between 'managerial' and 'professional' perspectives on teaching is similar to that in other public services. It has always been present in education, and has always been capable of being resolved. If the headteacher is accountable for what happens in the school, then we can expect attempts to be made to persuade staff to establish their basic intentions in line with those of the head. We can also expect that the nature of the work is such that success in achieving those intentions cannot be guaranteed! Nevertheless, if the teachers are all pursuing similar or congruent goals, then they will recognise similar kinds of outcomes as failures and successes, and look towards similar ways of achieving them. The fact that teaching does involve the exercise of judgement or discretion in the classroom, in the Lipsky/Young use of the term, far from making it inappropriate as an area in which 'management' can operate, actually increases the importance of middle management as a function, since it involves keeping the senior staff informed of what does and does not work, and where assistance is needed. However, as we shall see, carrying out this function is difficult in schools because of the cultural consequences of teachers' claim to be professionals.

SUMMARY

The argument put forward in this chapter is that contemporary government policy has strengthened the public accountability of schools and created a competitive environment in which teachers require assistance in creating the stability needed for them to do their job effectively. Providing such stability is a key task of leadership, but leaders need assistants who can promulgate the vision and values which the leaders wish the school to develop, and sustain those values through the daily work of teaching and other contact with pupils. They also need to take responsibility for informing the school's leaders of problems which are occurring, so that appropriate action can be taken to provide assistance. This view of middle management is uncomfortable when set against the claim which teachers make for professional status and the need for discretion to work effectively in the classroom, but the two views are not irreconcilable. Some kind of what can loosely be called 'middle management' is a necessary part of the operation of schools if they are to present a coherent and consistent image and service to the children, parents, and communities they serve, whether these be seen as consumers, clients, or in the pre-'market' sense of pupils and parents. We need now to consider in detail what 'management' involves, and how middle managers might carry out their tasks.

3

Middle Managers and the
Work of Management

KEY CONSIDERATIONS IN EXAMINING MANAGEMENT

An analytical approach to management theory allows us to identify a number of elements against which to consider writings and ideas. We can consider the functions which are needed in any organisation to facilitate its achievement of its 'primary task' – the key work which the organisation exists to carry out. Management theory tends to identify four different functions. 'Production' management deals with the basic work of the organisation, while financial management deals with the work of securing and allocating resources and ensuring that they are properly spent and accounted for. Marketing management is the work of ensuring that the production teams know what current or potential purchasers of the organisation's goods are wanting, their levels of satisfaction with what is currently produced, and the nature of the competition, and human resource management (formerly personnel management) is concerned with supporting and directing the people who are employed within the company, ensuring that the obligations created by employment law are met, that conditions of employment are satisfactory, and that staff generally are not discontented. In larger organisations, specialist managers focus on one or other of these functions; in smaller companies, people have to be generalists, dealing with several or all four functions. But even when managers have a specialist responsibility they are likely to have to be aware of the demands of all four areas. The concept of functions allows us to be aware that managers have to think about what the organisation does – in a school, teaching and learning; how it is funded, and how to spend what is available; how to persuade people to take up what is on offer; and how to motivate and support the colleagues with whom they work. Thus a head of English in a secondary school will have to consider, among other things, the nature of the curriculum, the quality of lesson preparation and teaching and the distribution of children among classes ('production'); the allocation of classes to teachers ('production' and human resources); the resource needs of the department, the ordering of materials, (resource/finance); reviewing the performance of both pupils and teachers ('production' again); and teacher motivation and ambition (human resources).

A second consideration that needs attention is the nature of the 'primary task' and the demands it makes of the people who do it. As was pointed out above, the demands of production management in a fast food outlet are different from those in a computer software house. Teaching and social work demand more discretion for the person dealing with the pupils and clients than routine manufacturing work on a production line, although some approaches to teaching require more than others.

Closely related to this is a third consideration, which is the extent to which the organisation's structure and its arrangements for monitoring and reviewing action relate to the work the organisation is set up to do. It is easy for structures to be created which do not work to the advantage of the people involved in carrying out the primary task, but which do work to the advantage of those who are supposed to be managing that work. This raises an important issue, which we examine in more detail later: that the process of organising work is itself a management activity, and that the structuring of work and the practice of management are intimately related (Hales 1993).

A last, but absolutely fundamental, consideration which we can take into account when studying management literature is the basic assumptions and values which the writers bring to bear on the problems they identify and the solutions they generate. In particular, these assumptions relate to how people are seen to be motivated and how it is expected the primary task will be completed. For example, a view of education as a mechanical production line towards defined outputs and of teachers as motivated entirely by personal gain would produce a different set of recommendations for management practice from a view which sees education as essentially a journey of discovery with no clear end-point and teachers as motivated by a love of knowledge rather than material gain.

It is possible to identify in the literature a number of schools of thought whose assumptions about the nature of work and the consequent responsibilities of managers are radically different, and who therefore produce quite different ways of thinking about management. In what follows we shall consider a number of these briefly, to point up differences and see how each approach alters our perception of middle management and the location of middle managers within the organisation.

Activity 3.1

Before we launch into an examination of writers, it would be a good idea to consider these four questions in relation to your own organisation. Who has responsibilities relating to which management functions? How do your duties relate to them? Does your view of the school's 'primary task' match up with the views of senior staff – and are these consistent? Does the school's organisation support the needs of those carrying out the 'primary task'? Are the values underpinning senior management practice in line with their stated perception of the work of teachers? A few minutes thinking about these will help you to relate what follows to your school, and test its applicability.

RATIONALITY, EFFICIENCY AND CONTROL: THE TRADITIONAL OR 'SCIENTIFIC MANAGEMENT' SCHOOL

The founding fathers of management theory are usually seen as F. W. Taylor (1911) and Henri Fayol (1949: first published 1915). Both engineers, their concern was with the demands of production management as large companies developed with long, highly mechanised mass production lines. Mechanised production techniques created a demand that all workers should operate the machinery in the same way, according to the instructions. There was thus one best way in which the machinery could be used, and therefore one best way in which the workers could operate to ensure maximum efficiency. This principle was then taken forward, and they developed quite independently from this starting-point a number of almost identical basic principles which, on the basis of a range of empirical studies of factory production work, they said could be established for organising manufacturing companies. These principles were then expanded into a general statement for all companies, and, by some other writers such as Bobbitt (1924), translated into other areas such as education.

By deriving the ideas of what managers had to do from the principle of one best way of organising work, these two writers created an essentially rational view of management, with a strong emphasis on efficiency, which has survived among many writers until today. The demands of mechanised production meant that the work of many different people had to be planned and organised, commands had to be given to carry out the plans, and the work had then to be co-ordinated. But Taylor also had a particular view of human behaviour which added another task. People, in his view, were motivated by self-interest and material gain. In any situation, they would do the minimum required of them. Therefore workers had to be employed under terms which would make it in their economic self-interest to produce as much as possible. Two things followed from this: payment by piece-rates or bonuses (the modern terminology is 'performance-related pay') and high levels of management supervision and control. Fayol itemised the consequent duties of managers as five fundamental tasks: planning, organising, commanding, co-ordinating and controlling, and most analyses of management work have been derived from this categorisation. Gulick and Urwick (1937) defined each of these elements as follows:

To plan means to study the future and arrange the plan of operations.

To organise means to build up material and human organisation of the business, organising both men (sic) and materials.

To command means to make the staff do their work.

To co-ordinate means to unite and correlate all activities.

To control means to see that everything is done in accordance with the rules which have been laid down and the instructions which have been given.

(Gulick and Urwick 1937, p. 119)

Gulick and Urwick, indeed, expand these five management tasks into seven: planning, organising, directing, staffing, co-ordinating, reporting and budgeting, or PODSCORB. This incorporates the functions of personnel and financial management into the model as specific management tasks, while the concept of 'control' has expanded to cover directing and reporting. Their view assumes some form of line of responsibility from the head of the organisation to the shop floor, because they derived from Taylor's approach three major requirements of all organisations: division of labour, span of control, and the 'principle of homogeneity'.

Division of labour is the requirement of breaking jobs down into their constituent parts to allow people to specialise. The consequence is supposed to be greater effectiveness of people in limited fields, but it increases the need for co-ordination. This in turn creates the need for a limited span of control for each person with supervisory or managerial duties, so that their co-ordination is effective: effectiveness is necessary at every level of the organisation. A rule of thumb developed that an individual could only oversee effectively the work of between five and ten other people, and in larger organisations this generated the pyramidal hierarchical structures which are so common. This development of small units of management gives rise to the third requirement: the basis upon which sub-units should be organised, or the principle of homogeneity. Gulick and Urwick suggested that people might be linked together because they have a common purpose (such as purchasing raw materials for all other departments), a common expertise (such as providing accounting services to purchasing), a common clientele or common raw materials (such as the sales force in north-west England), or a common location (such as an annexe away from the main company).

The basic assumption of this view of how organisations should be organised and run is that there is a rational relationship between the work and the workforce, and that this rational relationship can underpin its structure and operation. It further assumes that there is a straightforward relationship between ends or goals and the means to achieving them, and that therefore work can be planned in advance, and these plans can be met without difficulty. The manager's task is then to ensure that plans are carried through, controlling the output of individual workers and co-ordinating their work as necessary. The job of the worker is to carry out the specified tasks exactly in accordance with the rules or procedures laid down. Departures from the plan are to be avoided if at all possible, and another aspect of a manager's job is to minimise such departures and bring the workplace back to normal as soon as possible.

The other key concept in this view of management is control. Workers have to be kept adhering to the plan. The need to reduce individuals' span of control creates a need for levels of seniority within the organisation, and control has to be exercised at every level throughout the organisation. Management has to direct and command its subordinates and report on their progress to its superiors.

Although subsequent writers have called into question the narrow and mechanistic view of worker motivation which underpinned this 'scientific management' perspective, they did not for the most part challenge its central rational tenets. The human relations school, of whom the outstanding examples were Elton Mayo (1933) and Mary Parker Follett (Metcalf and

Urwick 1942), argued that attention needed to be paid to the needs of individual workers, who were not motivated merely by economic self-interest. Later writers, notably Herbert Simon (1948), have tried to fuse together the responsibilities for structure and human relations into a model which saw the manager as the maker of decisions which would affect the work of others, drawing on information which the organisation would collect about its environment. Simon also argues that managers can never take entirely rational decisions, because these must rest on total information, which can never be available. The best that can be done, he argues, is modified rationality or 'satisficing' behaviour – what looks best at the time. One must try to be rational, but acknowledge the limitations.

More recently, John Adair (e.g. 1983) has extended the discussion of human needs begun by Mayo and Follett, to distinguish between the department or team carrying out a task for the manager and the individuals in it. Just as the demands of the task and the needs of the people might not be in unity, so it is possible for an individual's needs to be at odds with those of the team as a whole. Adair argues that a key task of the manager is to be aware of such tensions and to manage them actively to try and produce the most satisfactory outcome from the point of view of the task, the team and each individual involved. However, when we analyse the managerial duties which Adair lists as being necessary for managing those tensions, we find a list almost identical with that of Fayol: defining the task, planning, briefing (i.e. ensuring that the team all know what they have to do), controlling, evaluating, motivating, organising and setting an example. Briefing would be unnecessary to the rigorous exponent of scientific management because rules and regulations would make it unnecessary, while motivating was seen purely as a matter of economic reward. Setting an example – a point which harks back to the discussion of leadership in Chapter 2 – is the only major new element Adair introduces which is not covered in traditional 'scientific management', either directly or in its assumptions and values. Table 3.1 demonstrates the similarities of these concepts of management responsibilities.

Table 3.1 Management responsibilities in the rational model

Fayol	Gulick and Urwick	Adair
Plan	Plan	Plan
Organise	Organise	Brief
Command	Direct	Control
Co-ordinate	Staff	Evaluate
Control	Co-ordinate	Motivate
	Report	Organise
	Budget	Set an example

The organisational consequences of this model of management have been indicated, but need some development. There is a strong correlation between scientific management and the development of hierarchical or pyramidal organisational structures, because of the need to sustain management control of all aspects of the work, including that of controlling others. There is therefore a danger that the demands of management control can finish up dictating the form of the organisation instead of this being determined by the demands of the primary task. There is also a clear tendency to distinguish between the sorts of work undertaken at each level, because the nature of the supervision will vary according to the task being supervised and the kind of information which is reported to the supervisor/ manager. As staff become more senior in the pyramid or hierarchy, they tend to acquire greater responsibility for planning and budgeting, and less for overseeing the detailed implementation of the plans, so that at senior level they leave the day-to-day details behind almost completely, focusing instead on longer-term and organisation-wide concerns. Thus it becomes possible to differentiate between the kinds of tasks, and the skills which are relevant to their performance, appropriate to each level of seniority. The enduring strength of this form of analysis is revealed by the thinking behind the British competency-based approach to management development called the Management Charter Initiative (MCI 1991), which distinguishes between junior/first line managers and middle managers, and sees middle managers as needing to be able to do everything a junior manager can do plus extra skills. However, the senior management 'standards' or competencies are quite different from those of other managers. Similarly, the competency model of Boyatzis (1982), which stimulated so much of the competency movement in management studies, differentiated sharply between what made good senior managers and the needs of those holding less elevated posts.

Activity 3.2

Do any of these ideas help you to think about your school and begin to understand how your responsibilities mesh with those of other staff? If you can, I suggest you identify three, and think about why they are helpful. My comments are in the appendix.

MANAGEMENT AS CREATIVE CONTROL: A SYSTEMS PERSPECTIVE

The basic assumptions of the scientific management school are that management is about control in a rational setting. However, it is possible to develop a different perspective by seeing organisations as systems which are capable, to a large degree, of controlling themselves. The systems perspective, which derives its thinking from the general systems theory developed by Bertalanffy (1973), sees organisations and the people in them as driven by a desire for self-preservation and maintenance. Once a system of work design and organisation is established, it will to a large extent run itself, and management does not have to worry about controlling it. Management need concern itself only with major breakdowns which the system cannot cope with, a principle sometimes called 'management by exception', and with longer-term review and goal-setting. This changes the balance of managerial activity from being essentially a controlling function towards being an enabling operation. Morris (1975) demonstrates the change in emphasis. He proposes that managers have four tasks:

- keeping things going, which involves ensuring that daily tasks are carried out satisfactorily. Since this can usually be done through standard systems and procedures, this need take very little time;
- coping with breakdowns, when something happens which the normal regulatory systems and procedures cannot deal with;
- doing new things, when for some reason it is found that the current range of activities carried out by the organisation is unsatisfactory; and
- keeping all the various tasks and activities under review and resolving tensions between them when they occur – bringing everything together into a coherent whole.

This view of management was taken up in relation to further education by Cuthbert and Latcham (1979), who identified five interrelated systems. System one was the basic work of teaching and learning: classroom and tutorial activity, with its attendant preparation and marking. System two was the control devices which kept system one functioning. The obvious element of this was the timetable, with its related rules such as the need to inform the timetabler in advance of known absences such as medical appointments. These two systems provided for the control devices and behavioural expectations which allowed the college to *keep things going*. System three represented the work which needed to be done when for some reason the other systems couldn't cope with a problem. For example, short-term staff absence could be covered by the timetabler through the use of cover staff, doubling up classes, or possibly calling upon supply teachers. However, if the absence were to be for a significant period, such as maternity leave, then it might be necessary to make a temporary appointment, which might involve other people in taking action. System three therefore monitors systems one and two and intervenes as necessary. It is not a control device, however: its purpose is to sustain smooth operation by *coping with breakdowns*.

If systems one, two and three represent day-to-day management, or keeping things going, systems four and five represent the last two of Morris' categories. System four is the planning and development function: trying to identify what is wanted of the college, reviewing client and customer satisfaction, and working to develop new course offerings and patterns of delivery which will satisfy existing and potential customers and generate more demand. It is important that this is seen as a more senior function, since it is possible for it to require changes in the day-to-day pattern of operation in some areas of the college – for example, if a department which has previously been operating on a traditional pattern of full-time students in classes and workshops, on the college site for twenty-five hours a week, finds that its numbers fall away, it might have to look for part-time students taking evening classes, or, more radically, to offering programmes of education and training off-site in the factories and offices of the firms which sponsored the students. Such a change could have considerable consequences both for the staff in the department concerned and for other staff in the college. Accordingly, the consequence of needing system four is the overarching broad policy-making level of the organisation: system five, which seeks to marry up the demands and pressures of keeping things going day-to-day and the implications of introducing the new things which are proposed. Thus system five balances the competing demands which the college faces and to which it must respond, decides on priorities, and allocates resources accordingly. It *brings it all together*.

Once again, this is an essentially rational view of management. Like the previous models, it differentiates between levels of seniority, and suggests that more senior managers, who deal with system four and, particularly, system five management, are likely to be more distant from the primary task of the organisation. However, it does not presume the same kind of structural rigidity as tends to derive from the more control-oriented scientific management approach.

Activity 3.3
Before going on to the next section, you might find it useful to consider the question, what do these views of how organisations operate and what managers have to do imply for the 'middle management' role? This is the subject of what follows.

SCIENTIFIC MANAGEMENT, SYSTEMS AND MIDDLE MANAGEMENT

There are both similarities and points of difference in the perception of the middle management role created by the two views of management outlined so far. From the point of view of scientific management, middle management is essentially about getting the job done, and being answerable for its achievement to some higher authority. What might be called 'classic' scientific management stressed the *control* dimension of this responsibility, whereas later writers such as Adair, who drew on the principles first articulated by Taylor and Fayol, have emphasised the importance of motivation and direction alongside that of control. By comparison, in the systems view of management, although middle managers still have the responsibility for getting the job done, there is a far stronger emphasis on the *facilitative* role: sorting out difficulties, ensuring that the system is running well, and creating procedures to ensure that it does.

What both scientific management and systems perspectives have in common is the importance they attach to managers knowing what is going on, either as reports for control purposes or as information for system-correction and the development of new ideas. This has significant implications for staff who hold positions between the performers of the primary task and those who are responsible for planning and bringing it all together. Middle managers perform a pivotal role in obtaining information, filtering it, creating priorities from it and ensuring that it is passed on to the proper destination. They are therefore well placed to create pressure for alterations to existing arrangements, and within the systems perspective may have flexibility within their areas of responsibility to change those arrangements.

This position as key brokers of information within the organisation adds an important dimension to the view of middle managers put forward in Chapter 2, as publishers of the vision of the organisation's leadership and the creators of systems through which it is achieved. They are also potentially agents of change through their ability to control and influence the flow of information in the organisation. If you consider the process of information gathering and dissemination from a rational perspective, particularly that which generates the idea of one best way of operating, this is not a problem, for the process of passing information through to one's superiors is a way of moving the organisation towards its optimal position. However, it may be that such a view of the middle manager depends on a traditional concept of the organisation for its validity. Burgoyne (1993) has pointed out that middle management posts are being removed more quickly in business and commerce than any other, because much of what they traditionally did can now be done through more sophisticated computer technology. For example, regional managers of chain stores are not needed to monitor the financial performance of each outlet: by courtesy of a computer terminal, the managing director can receive details of the performance of every store within thirty minutes of closing time, and can monitor the performance in microscopic detail. Mintzberg (1979) calls such a system the *divisionalised form*, and it may be more relevant to schools than it appears at first sight. However, in another recent study Frohman and Johnson (1993) argue that although middle managers are dissatisfied that their needs are not taken into consideration by senior staff when making policy, and that they do not have sufficient autonomy and authority to do the jobs they are expected to do, they still have a potentially powerful role to play as entrepreneurs and agents of change, largely because they are close to the workplace and can tell senior staff exactly what is going on.

Even so, the view of middle managers as the key source of assistance and information to their senior staff assumes that they share the goals and intentions of the bosses and will work loyally towards their achievement, as does the view that they are promulgators of the vision. Unfortunately, the world is not as rational as this view implies, and the potential exists for action by middle managers to be dysfunctional to the wider organisation, or even destructive. A non-rational perspective on the world also allows us to find other ways in which the middle manager may operate constructively as an agent of change, as Isabella (1990) suggests. In the work of Henry Mintzberg we find a management theorist who takes exactly this view.

CRITICISING THE RATIONAL VIEW OF MANAGEMENT: THE WORK OF HENRY MINTZBERG

We shall encounter Mintzberg's work in two ways. First, we shall look here at his examination of the nature of managerial work, in which he dismisses rational models as 'folklore' and develops an alternative perspective which allows us to introduce into this discussion a number of important new concepts. Later, we shall be revisiting his work to consider the implications of our view of management for organisational structures.

The starting-point of Mintzberg's argument (1990: first published 1975) is that the management tasks of planning, organising, co-ordinating and control are more like vague objectives that managers have when they are working than characteristics of their work. The view of managers as systematic, reflective planners, which comes through the work of Simon (1948) or Morris (1975), is a folklore. Few if any managers – even managing directors – have no regular duties to perform and constantly receive systematic and aggregated information upon which they can base rational, considered decisions in the progress towards the achievement of scientific management. Instead, he says, management consists of a mass of fragmented and disjointed activities, constant interruption, pressure for immediate answers to questions or solutions to problems, and a heavy reliance on word of mouth messages rather than measured and considered written memoranda and documents. If we study managers in action, then instead of reflective, systematic planning, we will find frantic and highly disjointed activity; instead of no regular duties, a range of activities which come upon a person by virtue of his or her office, such as receiving significant visitors if you are the headteacher or chief officer, or visiting key clients if you are a section head, rather than leaving these too-important contacts to a junior colleague. Aggregated information from computerised data banks is often less important than data from verbal sources such as conversations and phone calls with colleagues, which can give instant, informed, on-the-ground judgements about what is going on. As managers become more experienced, they will also come increasingly to value informal sources of information such as gossip, hearsay and speculation – what Mintzberg calls 'soft' information – because so much work as a manager involves trying to anticipate events rather than responding to them after they have happened. Mintzberg comments that the characteristic of much managerial work is immediacy, and today's gossip and speculation, especially from informed people, is often tomorrow's fact. Consequently, he says, 'the strategic data bank of the organisation is not in the memory of its computers but in the minds of its managers' (Mintzberg 1990, p. 166). This makes it difficult for managers to delegate much of their responsibility to others, since so much of what they do rests on their judgement and intuition – which rumours they choose to acknowledge rather than discount – rather than on any kind of observable scientific basis.

Having dismissed science and rationality as a basis for the work of managers, Mintzberg rests his alternative interpretation on two facts: that by virtue of their positions in an organisation, managers have had authority conferred on them over their unit or subunit, and this gives them some status. Formal authority and status, he claims, fashion particular kinds of social relationships, and within them managers play different roles at different times. Through their actions in playing out these roles they acquire information which enables them to take decisions on behalf of the unit. Mintzberg analyses ten roles, which he groups under three headings as follows:

Interpersonal roles:
Figurehead
Leader
Liaison

Informational roles:
Monitor
Disseminator
Spokesperson

Decision roles:
Entrepreneur
Disturbance handler
Resource allocator
Negotiator

The figurehead and leader roles are closely interrelated, since the first incorporates key ceremonial and formal tasks which it is important are carried out by significant members of the organisation (he gives as an example the president of a company who signs personally the letter to a school for disabled children which has asked for assistance with equipment for a particularly badly disabled child), while the second exerts both direct and indirect influence on the work of others. Mintzberg does not mention vision in this discussion of leadership, but interprets it as involving, among other things, motivating others and reconciling individual and organisational desires and expectations, which is closely connected to the points made about leadership in Chapter 2. The other interpersonal role is also important: it involves the contacts managers make with colleagues outside their unit, and Mintzberg claims that research shows that managers spend more of their time working with others outside their unit than they do with their colleagues inside it. (They also spend least time of all working with their superiors.) This liaison is the means by which they develop the informal network of contacts through which the crucial 'soft' information is gathered which keeps them one step ahead of the opposition. By opposition, he not only means outside competition for markets: we may face opposition from within our organisation, for example in our quest for resources. Thus the organisation as a whole is no more 'rational' than the work of the managers within it.

As we said above, this information is in Mintzberg's view what places managers at the centre of their organisational units, typically more knowledgeable than their subordinates even if not omniscient. They are both spokespersons for their unit into the wider organisation, and disseminators of information into their units.

The interpersonal and informational roles are major sources of the means to carry out the four decisional roles Mintzberg identified. As entrepreneurs, managers can initiate change, while as disturbance handlers they respond involuntarily to problems which arise in their units, such as the sudden illness of a key member. As resource allocators, they perform an absolutely crucial role, which is among their most influential, for resources are to be seen as more than just money and materials: Mintzberg points out that the distribution of work roles within a unit is an allocation of resources – consider, for example, how valuable a resource is represented to the timetabler by the classes any given member of staff likes (or does not like) to teach! The last decisional role is that of negotiator, which covers anything from smoothing over minor disagreements between colleagues to negotiating new contracts of employment or with potential suppliers.

Activity 3.4

Having read this alternative to 'scientific management', do you judge one perspective to be more realistic and helpful than the other? If so, are you able to identify any aspects of your job, or that of your section head or head of department, which you think need attention? My comments on the first part of this activity form the next section of the book.

Some of the roles suggested by Mintzberg are similar to those identified earlier. We can see echoes of systems four and three in the entrepreneurial and disturbance handler roles, for example, while the centrality of the informational roles is in accord with our earlier analysis. What is lacking are the assumptions of rationality and control: instead, management is presented as essentially judgemental and negotiative, involving the cultivation and creation of support networks through which the individual manager can operate. However, although Mintzberg identifies ten roles and underlines the intuitive nature of them, he is at pains to emphasise that they form an integrated whole, and that should any one be ignored the job cannot remain intact. He further suggests, in a commentary on his original paper published in the 1990 reprint, that it may be more helpful to see his view of management as another dimension of the work rather than a contradictory view of it. Thus, the Mintzberg view recognises the pressures created by human activity and attitudes and the complex nature of human motivation, and should be seen alongside, rather than instead of, the demands placed on managers by the need to deliver the 'primary task'. He suggests that the models outlined earlier emphasise the 'cerebral' or 'professional' face of management, whereas his approach emphasises the 'insightful' face. The difference between the two can be summarised as in Fig. 3.1.

It is clear from this table that Mintzberg places individual values at the heart of management action, and this is in accord with the argument of this book.

Insightful	Cerebral
Stresses commitment	Stresses calculation
Sees the world as an integrated whole	Sees the world as the elements of a portfolio
Uses a language which emphasises the personal values and integrity of the individual manager within the organisation	Uses the words and numbers of rationality

Figure 3.1   Insightful and cerebral faces of management
Source: Bennett 1992, p. 18.

However, he is also at pains to stress that while communication is a central task in the informational roles of monitor, disseminator, and spokesperson, 'communication' and 'information' are not simply written and spoken language and numbers. As his idea of figurehead and leadership roles clearly implies, there are other forms of communication which managers have to take account of. Individual behaviour has to conform to certain expectations deriving from office. Furthermore, the formal structure of the organisation informs its members of the values which are held within the company, school or whatever.

For this reason, it is important to pull in another aspect of social science which is increasingly being drawn on by management theorists: the concept of organisational culture. It is a key dimension of leadership theory, since, as Bryman (1992) makes clear, communicating a vision goes beyond simply stating a set of goals and a preferred route towards their achievement. It is also about communicating a set of values in a variety of ways. We shall consider the culture of schools in Chapter 4, but turn now to outline briefly some of the major aspects of the concept, since it is relevant to the idea of management and the role of managers which we are seeking to develop. It is also relevant to the discussion of organisational form with which this chapter will close, and which is another major theme of Chapter 4.

THE CONCEPT OF ORGANISATIONAL CULTURE

The concept of organisational culture is drawn from the sociological definition of culture, which sees it as the particular characteristics and forms of behaviour which distinguish one social, national or racial group from another. It can allow for large groups, both homogeneous and relatively heterogeneous, such as national groupings, and also for subgroups within cultures: within Scottish national culture, for example, we can recognise the strong Gaelic culture of the Western Isles which is quite different from that of Aberdeen. So it is, too, with organisational culture: we can talk of both the culture of the organisation as a whole and of distinct subcultures within it.

Organisational culture is frequently taken to mean, in everyday language, 'the way we do things around here' (Deal 1985; Fullan and Hargreaves 1992). This is a dangerous definition, however, for it can be taken to suggest that the relationship between the culture of an organisation and the people in it is a one-way influence, and that the culture is static. Most studies of organisational or societal culture see the relationship as a two-way process which allows individuals and groups to shape and alter the nature of the culture in which they operate. The culture of an organisation, therefore, cannot be regarded as static. This view of organisational culture is a crucial part of current management theory, because, as has been indicated several times, a key management task is seen to be the shaping of the organisational culture within which management responsibilities are exercised.

Organisational culture is communicated in a number of ways. It rests, ultimately, on a set of shared values which are created through interaction between individuals and groups. Although values can be shared, they are nevertheless held by individuals *as* individuals, and are initially created in a dialogue between ourselves and our circumstances. Young (1981, 1983) suggests that we create a hierarchy of fundamental values, taken-for-granted constructs which rest on those fundamental values, and rules-of-thumb which help us to order our actions day by day and moment by moment. It is suggested that the creation of shared values is a similar process, but involves contacts between us as individuals and the other group members as well as with our personal circumstances. This means that whereas our personal values can be private, our shared values must be to some extent public. However, once established they do not necessarily exist at a conscious or public level, and it is only when for some reason they are challenged that our underpinning cultural values become explicit. For example, it may only be when a child challenges our assumptions about what is appropriate classroom behaviour by being naughty in a repeated pattern that we might start to ponder why we approach issues of classroom discipline in the way that we do, or only when we have completely lost control of a class that we break through our belief that to ask for assistance is to admit to having 'failed' and so we get help.

From the underpinning values of the culture, groups derive standards of acceptable and appropriate behaviour for particular settings. These may be explicit formal *rules,* or implicit *norms,* which, though implicit, are not necessarily unstated, especially when breached. Both rules and norms can be powerful or weak, creating imperatives from which members depart at their peril. They are reinforced in public and private ways: as formal statements, rules have formal sanctions attached to them. Norms are enforced through forms of informal pressure or sanctions, and reinforced and made visible through activities which demonstrate or emphasise the forms of behaviour which are valued. These are usually referred to as *rituals* and *ceremonies.*

Writing about schools, Beare, Caldwell and Millikan (1989) suggest that cultures display different kinds of visible symbols of their underlying and intangible values, philosophy and ideology. Their argument rests on the formal and official symbols of school activity, and does not acknowledge the possibility that there might be alternative sets of values generating alternative symbols and meanings. These give rise to subcultures, which may be at variance with, and indeed in conflict with, the values and expectations of what is expressed as the formal and public culture of the organisation. However, in some of the symbols they identify they acknowledge ideas from writers on corporate culture such as Deal and Kennedy (1988) of ways in which managers can work to influence such cultures.

A number of 'conceptual/verbal symbols' identified by Beare, Caldwell and Millikan are obvious: the aims and objectives of the organisation have been mentioned before in connection with the key function of leadership. Also important are the language and metaphors chosen to express the aims and to describe the practice which should support them. Educational aims expressed in terms of market penetration and consumer choice bespeak a different set of values from aims expressed in terms of personal and human development and the fulfilment of individual potential. A school which declares its most significant achievements to be its examination passes indicates a different set of values from those of a school which stresses sporting and extra-curricular achievements. However, these expressions are open to 'misinterpretation' by those inside as well as outside the organisation. In 1993, the public school near my home acknowledged that 93 per cent of its pupils gained five or more GCSEs at grades A to C, but attempted to do so almost in passing: it was mentioned at the end of the Headmaster's address given to parents of year six children. Some of the parents present took this as being an admission that they ought to be able to do better, given that they could pick and choose their pupils from among those who could afford to pay the fees. Formal means of communication need to be backed up informally in order to ensure that the intended message gets across.

Two crucial means through which managers can work to develop a particular cultural perspective on the organisation and its work are the identification of 'heroes' in the organisation's history and the telling of stories which show up particular values which it is wished to stress. Deal (1985) tells of his experience with an American hotel chain, in which he was regaled with identical stories about its founder by a part-time waitress at Los Angeles airport and by senior executives at their annual residential convention and 'pep' rally which is a common feature of many medium-to-large American companies. It was clear to Deal that the stories were widespread throughout the company, and told to all levels of seniority the same message of particular values and behaviours which should be adhered to. He argues, therefore, that spreading the message through organisational stories is a significant task for managers to perform.

This task allows us, once again, to see middle managers as potentially a creative force within an organisation rather than merely a delivery mechanism. If they come to share the values which the leaders seek to establish as the basis of the organisational culture they wish to create, then middle managers can join in the task of bringing in change. This will help to establish what Martin and Meyerson (1988) have characterised as a culture of integration, in which norms are shared and strong group loyalty and coherence is created. However, it is also important to recognise that it is not *only* a management task: anyone, and ideally everyone, ought to be drawn into it. Both Nias, Southworth and Yeomans (1989) and Deal (1985) write of leaders needing the support of priests and heroes to support the work of the culture founder or aspiring deity. Deal's example of the waitress has already been mentioned. He also refers to an elderly and relatively junior member of staff in a company who has taken to himself the responsibility of keeping company traditions alive, and so is used, quite systematically, by senior staff and others committed to the company to ensure that appropriate messages are spread, stories told, and gossip generated. People apparently turn to him for verification of a range of stories and anecdotes which spread around the company.

However, not all cultures can be seen as integrative. It may be that a more common type is one in which dissonant values emerge, or, to pursue the religious analogies, heresies develop. The development or sustaining of alternative cultures within an organisation is typified as a culture of differentiation by Martin and Meyerson (1988), and where these occur managers have to deal with the consequences of norms which may operate in opposition to those which they are trying to create. They can also, of course, join the dissonant subcultures themselves, and this is a common phenomenon, especially when there is a change of leadership and attempts are being made to change the direction or culture of the company. The study of organisational cultures in schools by Nias, Southworth and Yeomans (1989), who explored attempts by headteachers to introduce what they called cultures of collaboration into primary schools, demonstrates the potential of promoted postholders both as supporters and priests of the intended cultural change and as standard-bearers of the opposition.

Martin and Meyerson (1988) also identify a third kind of culture: a fragmentation culture in which individual values do not coalesce enough to permit the creation of any kind of coherent overall culture, even one of a mix of subcultures. This is a concept more at a level of theory than observed in practice, although Meyerson (1991) has written up a study of a hospital psychiatric support service in these terms. The nearest example in relation to management and education, which will receive more attention in Chapter 4, is what Cohen and March (1974) call the garbage-can or ambiguity model of management. Bell (1989) has used this to study the development of a new school out of a three-way amalgamation, but his discussion suggests more a culture of differentiation than of fragmentation.

This outline of the concept of organisational culture has stressed the potential role of middle managers in developing, sustaining and altering the culture in which they operate. They can be leaders within their unit as well as supporters of the leadership (or counter-revolutionaries!) in the school. It will therefore come as no surprise to find that Bottery (1992) is uneasy at the idea of cultures being manipulated by managers in the direction of their own perceived goals. He claims that such action ought to rest on primary ethical questions rather than on what he calls second-order values. Fulop (1991) has commented in her study of entrepreneurship among middle managers in business that organisational cultures are control mechanisms. Schein (1983) comments that cultures are essentially devices for individuals to use when coping with forms of anxiety: they represent ways of creating security by reference to a public and shared set of values. This is the purpose of the 'social myths' which culture creates. Change therefore is always likely to be traumatic unless it can be achieved without challenging these central social myths, norms, rituals and symbols which communicate the underpinning cultural values. Anyone who has authority and status in the organisation can function either positively or negatively in seeking to uphold those existing cultural values, develop them, or work against change. As holders of formal authority and status, middle managers are in key positions to achieve what Isabella (1990) calls the cognitive shifts – the changes in ways of thinking – which may be necessary to bring about effective change.

ORGANISATIONAL CULTURE AND ORGANISATIONAL FORM

Organisational cultures sum up and embody the intentions of the dominant group or groups within them about both what the work is that they do and how it ought to be done, and operate through a variety of formal and informal control devices to keep their members in line. One important medium through which the culture is expressed is the form in which its members are organised. Handy (1993) has attempted to draw together organisational form and the values it expresses in his four-fold concept of cultures, which has acquired the status of a classic analysis, while Mintzberg (1979) has sought to differentiate empirically between different kinds of organisational forms, relating them to the kinds of work which they perform. In this sense, their analysis connects to Hales' (1993) point that how work is organised reflects the assumptions made about the nature of that work and how its needs can best be met.

Handy (1993) describes four kinds of organisational culture. For each he distinguishes between the form it takes, the basis on which influence is exercised over others, and the nature of interpersonal relations, and considers the settings in which they are appropriate. The four cultures are associated with *power, role, task* and *person.*

A power culture is best pictured as a web. All routes of influence flow to the centre, and the links between the radial lines are merely to secure the radials and stop them blowing away. All power is held at the centre and given out by the head in whatever ways that person sees fit. Such organisations are highly flexible, and well able to cope with uncertain environments, but only for as long as the person at the centre, who keeps all things dependent on him or her and is able to interfere in the work of others at a moment's notice, is properly informed as to developments. Since the head of the organisation retains all power and judgement at the centre, this can be difficult if the sources of information are not very good. On the whole, these are not well maintained by the people at other points in the web, since apparent challenges to the authority of the leader may lead to rapid dismissal. A consequence of this is often very rapid turnover of staff. Entrepreneurial activity and individualism is accepted as long as the person doing it is approved of: others will be disciplined for it.

A role culture is depicted as a Greek temple. It is in many respects the opposite of the free-floating web, being rigid and clear. Everyone has a defined role which is linked clearly to everyone else. Decisions are taken by senior staff, who live in the temple pediment, and pass instructions down the pillars of the temple. There, the carefully defined work is separated into specialist areas, thereby enhancing the importance of the overview achieved by the senior staff. Communication is usually formal and written, unlike that of the web/power culture, where much rests on word of mouth. It is essentially a rule-driven culture, good for stable settings and environments, and in those circumstances providing a secure basis from which to operate, but it is difficult to change quickly, and places a low premium on individuality and entrepreneurship.

A task culture is more flexible than a role culture in that its membership is restructured in order to complete each new task or project which is taken on. Individuals have particular specialisms, and these are drawn together under a project leader and then reassembled when that project is completed. Handy portrays it as a net, with stronger and weaker connections depending on whether the relationship between individuals indicated by the net is more or less permanent. The existence of a network of interrelationships demonstrates both the potential strength of the organisation, with its many interconnections, and the degree of openness and collaboration which exists within it. Senior management has a less directive role here: there will be somewhere a decision-making responsibility on which projects to accept, but thereafter the project leaders will develop and monitor progress in conjunction with the clients for whom the project is undertaken. Handy comments that this is a culture which prospers in times of expansion but has great difficulty coping with contraction: then, senior management tends to try and increase its control, and there is a tendency to move back towards a role, or even a power culture.

Handy's last cultural form is the person culture. This he depicts as a cluster of stars, with no obvious connections between them. It is characterised by an insistence on individual autonomy and a resistance to any leadership being exercised by anyone. Everything is a matter of protracted negotiation. As a culture it is to be found in organisations such as barristers' chambers or some smaller consultancy partnerships. However, Handy suggests that such cultures tend not to outlive their founders, since organisations tend to take on a life of their own, which starts the move towards a different kind of culture. It is worth pointing out that Bryman (1992), in his study of charismatic leadership, refers to Weber's argument that charismatic organisations will eventually bureaucratise, which will take them towards a form of what Handy has called a role culture.

Handy comments that each type of culture is relevant to particular circumstances and kinds of work. He also points out that particular types seem to be favoured by people in particular circumstances or from particular backgrounds. Middle managers and professionals, for example, tend to be most favourably inclined towards a task culture: it gives maximum freedom of action and discretion, and places their expertise at a premium. Experts are given a largely free hand, and the middle manager (usually a project manager or director) is effectively a free agent, reporting to the directorate only in terms of the proper use of the finances and the completion of a satisfactory report. Echoes of this will be found in the last of Mintzberg's organisational forms, which he calls the divisionalised form.

Mintzberg (1979) offers a categorisation of organisations which has similarities to that of Handy, but is structured rather differently. He identifies five kinds: simple, adhocracy, machine bureaucracy, professional bureaucracy and divisionalised form. The *simple* form is similar to the power culture, with all decision-making authority being concentrated at the centre. An *adhocracy* is similar to the task culture, being reorganised on the basis of the needs of a particular project and client. Mintzberg sees these as being unable to develop effectively, since the continuous rearrangement of membership makes it difficult to transfer techniques and skills of collaborative working from one project to another since one is working with a different group of people, and so has to start the process of negotiating relationships all over again. He comments that adhocracies tend to be 'young' organisations, which bureaucratise with age towards role cultures, or, as he calls them, *machine bureaucracies*. These are co-ordinated by the demands of standardising the work process, and permeated by rules and regulations. The only people who are free of the dictates of the standardised procedures which are created and controlled by the senior staff are the technical staff who, by their very nature, have to be able to investigate the way the work process is operating and try to make improvements. Most managers outside the senior levels have little freedom of action: indeed, first line managers can often find their job is so circumscribed that they can hardly be said to be managers at all.

So far, Mintzberg's forms reflect Handy's analysis, but thereafter he goes his own way. He does not acknowledge the person culture, but offers two others instead. The *professionalised bureaucracy* is in many ways a development of the task culture, but takes account of the issues outlined by Lipsky (1980) concerning the nature of professional work and its competing needs for efficient operation. It is highly decentralised, and focused on what Mintzberg calls the 'operating core' and the people who work there, rather than on a larger controlling or organising structure. Co-ordination is achieved through the common skills and knowledge possessed by those at the core, but a great deal of latitude is allowed in their work, so that there is no great need for lateral communication. The prevailing mode of operation is through consultation with the individual client, while recognising that in most cases this process will lead to the client being categorised for some kind of standard treatment. By placing responsibility for deciding what is to be done at the point of action rather than at some more senior position, this organisational form is, in Mintzberg's view, highly democratic. Where the actor refers the case to another person, it is for expert opinion rather than because of senior status. Mintzberg suggests that this is the dominant mode of organisation in social work agencies, hospitals and universities, and proposes that the school system in the USA and Canada (the equivalent of the LEA in the United Kingdom) can also be seen in these terms, with the schools being the decentralised and significantly autonomous operating cores, possessed of considerable discretion.

Mintzberg's last organisational structure is called the *divisionalised form*. In this form, the headquarters of the company reorganises the work into a number of divisions, each of which can address a particular market, and reduces to a minimum the number of functions and activities carried out by the headquarters staff, which is greatly cut back. Each division is, in Mintzberg's words, 'a set of quasi-autonomous entities coupled together by a certain administrative structure' (Mintzberg 1979, p. 381). Headquarters co-ordinates the work of the divisions by establishing strict financial controls, and by attempting to standardise outputs in some way. This is usually financial, such as return on investment or profit. Divisional managers therefore plan so that the work of their staff is geared towards the performance goals laid down by headquarters. However, it is not a decentralised system, for it does not place decision-making at the point of action: instead, 'it constitutes the vesting of considerable decision-making power in the hands of a few people – the market unit managers in the middle line, usually at the top of it – nothing more' (Mintzberg 1979, p. 104).

The divisionalised form is essentially a form of large organisations and companies. It bears strong similarities to English and Welsh LEAs after the introduction of LMS, and to the relationship between Grant Maintained Schools and their Funding Agency or Council. These fund their individual schools – divisions – on the basis of their success in gaining pupils (age-weighted pupil formulae) and monitor their achievement through the data they must submit on pupil enrolment and their output as recorded in league tables. It is possible to conceive of headteachers, rather than the holders of incentive allowances, as 'middle management' within the system – a view which will not gain much support from the heads! However, even if we do take this view, we still need to examine the internal workings of each division in order to unravel what is happening to the management there, since considerable variety can develop between divisions, and, indeed, between subunits of smaller organisations.

Involved in many of the organisational forms outlined here is the concept of decentralisation. This is of great importance when thinking about the work of middle management. Mintzberg (1979) distinguishes usefully between two different kinds of decentralisation: it can be horizontal or vertical, and it can be selective or parallel. Vertical decentralisation is the most obvious: delegating authority down the line to a more junior level. Horizontal decentralisation is a rather different idea, concerning the extent to which authority is dispersed away from the traditional line management arrangement towards others, such as advisers or technical staff. The extent to which this is done can seriously affect the degree of authority and discretion available to a middle manager, who derives all authority from the position which was granted by senior staff. Selective decentralisation occurs when only certain powers are delegated and others retained. Almost all vertical decentralisation is selective, since by its very nature senior management has to retain certain authority – otherwise it is unable to fulfil the functions it exists to do. The alternative form of decentralisation Mintzberg identifies – parallel decentralisation – is when a lot of decisional authority is dispersed to the same place. The authority of the divisional heads in divisional form organisations would be a good example of this.

In outlining the ideas of Handy and Mintzberg on organisational culture we have tended to assume that they are cultures of integration, and have passed over possible sources of dissonance which might lead to cultures of differentiation. However, there is plenty of room for such diversity to develop, both between divisions in large organisations and within them, and within smaller organisations too. In particular, it is quite possible to find a combination of task and role cultures in place side by side, with the formal organisation operating as a role culture and individual units within that culture functioning more as task cultures. At one school I researched, it was possible to identify a clear role culture at the level of overall organisation, and in the relations between heads of department and senior staff. Within individual departments, however, it was possible to find both strong task cultures, in which a high degree of collaboration and sharing took place and jobs were completed according to who was interested and able to take them on, and strong person cultures, in which individual teachers did entirely their own thing and refused to co-operate on a systematic basis with anyone.

Hales (1993) has also demonstrated that managers in bureaucratic organisations, which he analyses in ways which equate with Handy's role culture, often attempt to reform and loosen the rules and hierarchical expectations by introducing 'task forces', but these task forces then find that their ideas and attempts at reform are blocked by those managers who rest their authority on the existing bureaucratic structure. An example of this at a secondary school was the experience of a curriculum development working party created by a newly appointed head. Its members became increasingly frustrated because most of the time at meetings was spent in discussing the head's criticisms of their previous discussions. In the end, the head of technology asked the deputy head chairing the meetings if the head would mind telling the task force what he wanted them to say so that they could stop meeting and get on with doing something useful. He wasn't popular!

Activity 3.5

The concept of organisational culture is, in my view, extremely important. If you are concerned to try and establish what your job requires of you, then you should attempt to undertake some cultural analysis of your own school. You should ask the following questions:

1. Using either the Handy or Mintzberg typology, how would you characterise the culture of your school?

2. Within what we might call that structural aspect of the culture, is it a culture of integration, differentiation or fragmentation?

3. What aspects of school activity communicate the messages that lead you to these conclusions?

4. To what extent do you identify a difference between the overall school culture and that within your area of responsibility (or your main area of work)?

5. What expectations can you identify people as holding of you in your management position? How do these expectations communicate themselves to you?

6. In so far as there are conflicts between those expectations, and between them and your own expectations of yourself, how do you resolve them?

7. To what extent do you feel constrained or restricted in the actions you can take by the cultural norms of the school?

CULTURE, FORM AND ORGANISATIONAL SIZE

It was indicated above that divisionalised form organisations tended to be large companies rather than small ones, and the examples Handy offers of person cultures are small units such as barristers' chambers. This raises the question of size, which is relevant to our thinking about organisational culture, and an important consideration when thinking about middle management. It can be argued that we must have organisations of a reasonable size before we can even conceive of the idea of 'middle management'; certainly the companies most heavily involved in developing the Management Charter Initiative (MCI), which distinguishes between first-line and middle management competencies and assumes a career progression from one to the next, were large rather than small. A number of points may be made here, some of which may seem obvious but are often overlooked, and are relevant to the discussion in the chapters which follow.

Smaller organisations are more likely to possess unitary or integrationist cultures. It is not simply that there are fewer people involved, and so fewer chances for disagreement and opposition; there are also fewer places in which people can meet away from the main body of their colleagues, and fewer specialists who can stress their importance. When everybody is a generalist, it can be proposed that there is more likelihood of co-operation.

Smaller organisations also have less reason to move towards role or bureaucratic cultures. More can be done informally, and fewer rules are needed. However, this is not to deny that in many cases small organisations have to meet external demands for records and standards of performance which create a need for forms of administrative machinery and record-keeping. This might be ensuring that production tolerances are within British Standard specifications for a customer; it can also be ensuring that pupil records are in order. We have to remember, in the case of schools, that although they have substantial autonomy under local management or by becoming grant maintained, their autonomy is over how they do what they are charged with doing rather than over what they do. Thus even small primary schools might be thought of as small units within a large, divisionalised, organised organisation called the national state education system.

By comparison, larger organisations have much more room for developing differentiation or even fragmentation cultures. Their staffing numbers have to be organised, and there is more likelihood of specialist skills being recruited. There is more room for failure to meet specifications or standards, and so more need for monitoring, if not control. There are more people with whom to develop alternative subcultures, and more places in which to do it. The existence of specialist employees can change how the work is organised: there is no intrinsic reason why children in year six should be taught by one teacher for all (or almost all) aspects of the curriculum, but the same children in year seven meet seven or eight teachers each week, except that the school attended in year seven has teachers who have specialised in particular subjects and teach them at more advanced levels.

The above example demonstrates that the nature of the work done is clearly affected by the structure and size of the organisation and the composition of its employees. It also makes clear that the culture of the organisation can both affect and be affected by the nature of the work. Subject specialists create a particular form of school organisation, which creates a particular administrative arrangement for allocating teachers to classes. This affects the nature of the 'middle management' function: how it is defined, what sorts of accountabilities exist, its relations with other middle managers, the degree of independence or autonomy of the unit managed compared to other units, and so on. By comparison, generalists create a different arrangement, and a quite different middle management function.

SUMMARY

This chapter has established a number of points. First, it has demonstrated that management theory is not monolithic, and can recognise the crucial importance of the work done by an organisation, and that this can have a bearing on how it is organised, what values it is wished to embrace in working there, and what managers might do to promote those values in the process of getting the work done. It has offered views based on rationality and control, which tends to make management a delivery mechanism; rationality and the development of largely self-regulating systems so that management can become a more creative, facilitative process; and management as a creative, intuitive and judgemental process, which rests on the importance of the individual colleagues with whom the manager works. Each generates a quite different view of what the management function is and what managers need to do to carry it out.

Secondly, it has identified a range of different cultural characteristics and related organisational forms which communicate the underlying values which the organisation's members wish to embrace and project. In emphasising both formal and informal means of influencing the ideas of others, it has stressed that managers are not alone in exercising forms of influence, even if they are the only staff accorded formal authority, but that they, too, can operate informally to achieve the values they wish to create. It has also demonstrated the pivotal role of middle managers as creators of culture, communicators of the vision, and generators and facilitators of change.

Lastly, it has related management values, the management task, and issues of organisational form and culture to the issue of size, and indicated that all three combine to affect the middle management role profoundly. This is as true of schools as of any other organisation. Small companies do not operate in the same way as multinational conglomerates; two-teacher rural primary schools do not function like urban comprehensives with over one hundred teachers, a range of ancillary staff, and two thousand pupils, and neither is the same as the large technical college with its heads of department, each of whom has a budget larger than most secondary schools and responsibility for a range of courses in a variety of modes, often dependent on a raft of part-time teachers to ensure that they can be delivered.

The work of a middle manager, then, is affected by a variety of considerations. We have explored them in relation to management in general, but we have not yet considered in detail the processes which are involved in trying to do the job. There are a number of approaches which have been identified in the literature. Some are strongly normative and prescriptive, offering direction as to what managers ought to do, while others claim to be representations of how things really happen. It is when we get to this stage of our analysis of the role and work of managers that it is important to locate our discussion in contexts which are readily transferable to the reader's own setting. In Chapter 4 we shall look at theories of management practice in relation to education.

4

Schools and Management

We will look at management in schools by focusing on two major themes. The first is to identify the kinds of cultural norms and expectations which can characterise schools and influence their organisational forms. Then we shall consider how managers might organise the work of the school and think about their own work. Before this, however, we need to ask how it is that these cultural norms influence how people act.

IDEAS AND ACTION: 'ASSUMPTIVE WORLDS', 'ESPOUSED THEORIES' AND 'THEORIES IN USE'

Management literature often distinguishes between subjective values and objective behaviour. Young (1981) suggests instead that our thoughts and actions are indissolubly interconnected. How we act is shaped by what he calls our 'assumptive world', which is not a static set of ideas, but something we construct actively by taking 'facts', ascribing values to them, and trying to make sense out of them so that we can establish an understanding of how we relate to the world around us. Out of this process comes a fourth dimension, which impels us to act directly in relation to the world as we perceive it. Thus we might take a range of facts and opinions, including information which we cannot verify but are prepared to accept as true, and identify some as more important than others in the light of our existing beliefs. This creates a sense of what is right and good for a particular setting, and so allows us to decide whether we need to act, and if so, how. Young suggests that this active process of construction and reconstruction produces a hierarchical structure of values and beliefs. Low-level beliefs or precepts – for example, that in response to seeing two children fighting in the playground I should go and stop the fight – draw their validity from an appeal to what he calls 'middle range' constructs, which we use to manage the world as we have currently constructed it. These 'middle range' constructs are themselves drawn from symbolic, generalised, taken-for-granted fundamental values, often assertions, that suffuse our everyday actions and experience. Middle range constructs can be revisited quite frequently and amended, but the symbolic values are only revisited in extreme circumstances (Young 1981, p. 42). Thus we have a subjective understanding of the situation. If we fuse this together with the action we take in that situation, we have, says Young, a better understanding of how we deal with the world around us, by defining a 'life space' or 'action space' in which to operate.

A rather different but related idea comes from Argyris and Schon (1978). They suggest that in any situation it is possible to identify two sets of guiding principles influencing individual action. There will be the publicly stated 'espoused theory', through which the individual lines up what is going to be done with official policies or widely shared and acknowledged cultural norms. There will also be the private 'theory in use', which will be the real guiding principles behind what actions are actually taken. These may be identical, but it is equally possible for them to be at odds with each other: a teacher might 'espouse' publicly the school's formally stated philosophy of child-centred discovery learning but operate in the classroom on traditional, didactic lines. Young's 'assumptive world' allows for this: in a public setting this teacher might feel obliged to declare support for certain principles but find it impossible to carry them out in the classroom. Various actions will then flow from the perceived need to justify or conceal the discrepancy.

Activity 4.1

To test these ideas, it might be helpful to review, privately (and entirely honestly!), what happened in a recent incident in which you reacted to events quickly. Why did you act as you did? Did it give you reason to think afterwards about whether what you did was correct? Are you satisfied that you acted properly and in accordance with your principles?

You might also ask yourself if you can identify an occasion when you have publicly supported one course of action but actually pursued another in your teaching or dealings with others; and if there has been an occasion when you have found yourself feeling obliged to act in a manner contrary to formal or official school policy.

I confess all in the appendix!

In what follows, we look at three important aspects of our work as teachers which have a significant influence on how we approach our managerial role. It is argued that just as issues such as school size, location, intake and age of pupils create differences between schools, so there are differences in the way we think about teaching, about the knowledge base of our teaching which creates our authority in the classroom, and in our perception of what is proper behaviour in our teaching and school life, which affect our stance towards our colleagues and our view of what is likely to be acceptable and effective managerial action.

CULTURES OF SCHOOLING 1: OUR VIEW OF TEACHING

Although teachers share a common accountability to parents and governors, and through their governors to central government, for discharging their teaching duties, this commonality does not last long once we start exploring how they think about their actions to meet that accountability. In the first place, teachers of young children see their work differently from teachers of older pupils. The classic distinction between the answers to the question, 'What do you do?' is still common: primary school teachers are likely to answer, 'I am a junior/infant teacher,' while secondary teachers are more likely to answer, 'I teach history/physics,' or 'I am a head of house.' This indicates a clear difference between their perceptions of what their job involves, and what they are responsible for. It is not a difference between being specialists and generalists, although primary teachers have to be competent in a range of subject areas, whereas secondary school subject specialists do not. The work of a primary teacher, handling thirty children of a particular age and embracing a particular range of developmental achievement, is just as much specialist work as that of a subject specialist, teaching a subject to a wide range of ages and abilities throughout the secondary and maybe the post-sixteen sector.

When we look at the work involved in being a primary teacher or teacher of a secondary school subject, we find more differences within each category. A reception class teacher faces different demands from those faced by a year six teacher in the same school, and teaching a year seven class creates different demands from teaching year ten GCSE students. Large groups require different approaches from small groups, classes consisting substantially of children for whom English is a second language have different needs from those of a class consisting entirely of mother-tongue children, and so on.

Not only do individual classes place different demands on their teachers, but the ways teachers respond to them are different. Wise *et al.* (1984) have suggested that we can view the work involved in teaching children in four ways: as *labour*, as *craft*, as *profession*, or as *art*. Each creates different sets of demands for the teachers to meet and their managers to attend to, and affects the nature of the relationship between them.

If teaching is seen as *labour*, it involves following set plans and procedures. Course programmes are established, the exercises and tasks required of the children identified, and all the assessment arrangements predetermined. Teachers will cover the exercises in a specified way, using laid-down teaching strategies, and sticking to a clear schedule. Their job is not to innovate or adapt the scheme, but to deliver it: the business of writing the scheme or syllabus and deciding what is to be taught and how, is not part of the teacher's responsibilities. Further, they will be supervised closely in carrying out the work. Teaching as labour sees the teacher as a production line worker in a traditional, machine-based factory, and assumes that effective practice which will produce the desired results if adhered to can be concretely determined and specified.

Labourer-teachers, according to Wise *et al.*, have to be *supervised*. That is to say, they must be monitored and observed closely in action, and assessed by reference to predefined standards of both practice and outcome. The management functions emphasised in this view of teaching are those of planning and control.

By comparison, teaching as a *craft* involves acquiring a range of specialist techniques, and learning general rules about how and when they should be employed. Teachers work without close supervision once they have been given their assignment, because it is assumed they are competent, but they do not have any say in what that assignment should be. They still work to clearly laid-down expectations of what they will teach, what will be learnt, and what forms of assessment will be employed. Teaching viewed as a craft, then, is a repertoire of skills and techniques which make teachers basically competent to operate independently on predetermined tasks. It assumes that general rules can be developed and that knowledge of these and of the techniques will produce the required results.

Craft-teachers are *managed*. That is, they are held accountable for results, but not for the methods employed unless the results are unsatisfactory. They are only subjected to close supervision if they fail to meet the standards required. Key management functions in this perspective are planning, organising and co-ordinating the work.

Teaching as a *profession* requires the teacher to go beyond the exercise of craft skills to diagnose problems, evaluate possible responses and adopt a chosen course of action. Wise *et al.* argue that being able to exercise such judgement depends on the possession of sound theoretical knowledge as well as technical skills, and that it must be supported by agreed standards of understanding and competence which can be justified by reference to theory. Enforcement of those standards will produce the required results.

Such professional teachers are not subject to management, but are supported by *administration*. Administrators ensure that adequate resources are provided, and discharge the management functions of organisation, co-ordination and budget. Evaluation of performance is carried out by professional peers, and a head of department, say, can only assess colleagues' work by virtue of her/his professional qualifications and status. Such a co-professional could also exercise Adair's (1983) management function of setting an example.

Teaching as an *art* is essentially a personalised view of teaching. It does not deny the importance of techniques nor of standards of practice, but because teaching rests on individual, personal understanding of what is needed for a particular setting, those techniques may be deployed in novel and unconventional ways. Rules and procedures give way to intuition, creativity, improvisation and expressiveness. The teacher as artist, then, has to rely on personal insight as well as theoretically grounded knowledge, and therefore requires considerable autonomy and discretion in order to function effectively.

The artist-teacher is not managed at all, but is led and encouraged. Once again, the results are all that are assessed. The only management function acknowledged, if any, is that of budget.

The characteristics of each perspective are set out in Table 4.1.

Clearly, the relationship between the individual teacher as class teacher and the colleague as head of department, curriculum co-ordinator, or other 'middle manager' will be affected by the view of the teacher which each side takes.

Table 4.1 Wise *et al.*'s (1984) four perspectives on teaching

Perspective	Key elements	Management relations	Management functions acknowledged
Labour	Follow set plans and procedures exactly	Close *supervision* of practice as well as outcomes	Planning Control
Craft	Possesses specialist skills and techniques Follows general rules of practice Works to clearly laid-down expectations of what will be taught	*Management* by results Procedures and techniques employed will be checked if results unsatisfactory	Planning Organising Co-ordinating
Profession	Possesses specialist skills and techniques Able to diagnose problems and identify solutions Strong theoretical grounding for work	*Administration* provides support and resources Evaluation of performance by peer professionals	Organising Co-ordinating Budget (Setting an example)
Art	Techniques deployed in novel and individualistic ways Judgement of appropriate practice both individualistic and unique	*Leaders* encourage the artist to perform Evaluation by results or outcomes	Budget

Only if both sides agree about the view of teaching which should underpin their practice is the relationship likely to be smooth. Nor should it be assumed that problems are only likely to arise if the 'manager' sees teaching work as requiring more supervision than the teacher. It is obvious that a teacher who sees her work as requiring the discretion to exercise her professional judgement while her manager sees it as a classroom craft which assumes the application of general rules, will find the supervision exercised over her work repressive and constraining. But a teacher who sees his work as a craft while his manager sees it as an art will also be unhappy because the leadership she offers will not give him the guidance and direction he feels he should receive.

Public statements by the Department for Education and the Chief Inspector for Schools (e.g. Woodhead 1995) indicate a move by central government in

England and Wales towards the clear specification of acceptable teaching methods. This suggests that teaching is being seen more as a craft or even as labour, with consequent changes in the kinds of supervision and control which will be required of teachers' classroom work. Government initiatives to create school-based schemes of initial teacher training – not, be it noted, education – give further support to this view, as did the articled and licensed teacher schemes. All these initiatives systematically play down the place of theoretical knowledge in the training process, making professional status that much harder to justify.

Against this, the rhetoric of teacher unions, teacher trainers and teacher staff-room conversations is a rhetoric of teachers as professionals. Ribbins (1992) comments that it may be seen as a 'folk term', an aspiration to a vaguely understood status attributed to other groups who may be regarded as professionals and who are seen to be more respected socially – and better rewarded – than ourselves. In this 'folk' language, 'professionals' such as doctors and lawyers are ascribed high social esteem and incomes because they possess esoteric knowledge barred to outsiders, regulate their own recruitment, training and standards of conduct, and can refuse the right to practise to those who fail to meet them (Becker 1962). They are also believed to work as autonomous individuals not subject to direct supervision (Ribbins 1992). Although few professions come anywhere near this ideal in practice it is understandable that teachers, faced with increasing restrictions on their autonomy, consumerist pressures from central government and a sustained public attack on their competence, should aspire to such status.

It is clear, then, that we can find a variety of perceptions of the work of a teacher, depending on the kinds of children being taught, the responsibilities held, and the fundamental concept of teaching. How this set of perceptions comes together will influence an individual teacher's attitude towards the children taught, the teaching colleagues who share the staffroom, and the parents and wider community who have dealings with the school. It will affect how they see these others, how they respond to actions, and how they act to take initiatives. It will affect what they see as legitimate action in a particular setting – what an individual's obligations to others are – and in particular, when they see it as acceptable to take an initiative. Consider, for example, this incident. I was waiting in a primary school playground one afternoon to collect my sons, and there was a lot of horseplay developing among the pupils waiting for the coach which would take them back to another part of the town. The duty teacher was clearly delayed, so I intervened to end the horseplay before one of the younger children got hurt. When the teacher came out a few minutes later, he was clearly angry that I had started to do his job for him, and snapped angrily at me, 'I'll take over now.' Was this because I was a parent usurping his authority over the children? Whatever the reason, his view of his responsibilities and mine was such that what I had done was unacceptable behaviour.

Our perception of teaching, then, forms a key dimension of our assumptive world by influencing what we will regard as acceptable and unacceptable actions on our own part and behaviour by others. It affects both our espoused theory and our theory in use. It is therefore a key determinant of the school's culture, in that it will influence the norms which shape informally what we do. But as Chapter 3 demonstrated, the difference between individual perceptions and organisational culture is that the culture is shared. This discussion has shown that it is likely that there can be disagreements between members of staff of any school about fundamental expectations, and this will have an impact on the degree of unity and coherence of the school's culture. This suggests that cultures of differentiation may be more common in schools than cultures of integration: we may have to identify subcultural forms.

Activity 4.2
It would be a useful exercise to apply the Wise et al. typology to your colleagues' view of teaching, and your own. If you are in a secondary school, to what extent do the members of your department agree? Do you find a similar agreement between the members of any other team you belong to – year or house tutors, for instance? Can you identify any teams or departments within the school which are either fully in agreement or totally at variance over their view of teaching? In a primary school, are there any groups of teachers who agree on a particular perspective different from others?

CULTURES OF SCHOOLING 2:
THE KNOWLEDGE BASE OF OUR THINKING

As well as our view of teaching, the type of knowledge which underpins our view of the world is also important in shaping the nature of our organisation's culture. Different perceptions of the world can create quite different expectations. Sackmann (1992) has suggested that it is possible to distinguish between four types of knowledge at the core of organisational cultures, each of which tends to generate different organisational forms. She identifies *dictionary* knowledge, or knowledge of *what* is to be done; *directory* knowledge, which is knowledge of *how* it is to be done; *recipe* knowledge, identifying how things *should* be done; and *axiomatic* knowledge, which states *why* things are to be done in the way that they are. These forms of knowledge bear a relationship to the typology of teaching put forward by Wise et al. (1984). Directory knowledge – a coherent and agreed view of how things must be done – relates clearly to the labour or craft views of teaching. Sackmann found that clear rules and procedures tended to create integrated cultures and hierarchical, 'rational' management styles. Recipe knowledge allied to dictionary knowledge relate to teaching as a profession, and are likely to create differentiated or even fragmented cultures, or, put another way, a multiplicity of subcultures. Axiomatic knowledge tended to be the basis of strong senior management groupings in organisations, along with a clear idea of who were 'the right kind of people' for the company. Sackmann suggested that this tended to fuse together dictionary and directory knowledge. Once again, it is likely to generate strong rules and requirements – a role culture or professional bureaucracy –

unless the consequence of strong axiomatic knowledge exercised over a long period of time creates a uniform recipe knowledge as well as directory knowledge.

If we link the idea of different kinds of knowledge, emphasising different aspects of our understanding, with our earlier discussion of assumptive worlds, it becomes possible to see the management task as trying to create a consensus around the kinds of knowledge which underpin an organisation. Axiomatic knowledge – the 'why' of practice – which fuses together in its sense of 'right' people knowledge of 'what' is to be done and 'how', is likely to be the most easily directed organisation. The kind of leadership and vision which we discussed earlier will thrive best if the axiomatic knowledge of the senior staff can be married up with the directory knowledge of the staff as a whole – assuming this is to be found.

This may sound unnecessarily complex, but it can be very helpful in distinguishing between teachers' views on the academic content of their work and what they regard as acceptable methods of teaching it, although the two are linked. Researching secondary schools to examine the impact of external curriculum policies immediately prior to the establishment of the national curriculum in England and Wales (Bennett 1991), I found a clear culture of the autonomous, independent teacher. It was not appropriate to talk about problems of teaching or classroom discipline in the staffroom except to a small group of personal friends whom you trusted – as one teacher put it, it was unwise to be too open, and impossible to be too quiet. Although senior staff could admit to bad lessons and disasters, this example was not followed by others. In terms of directory knowledge – how to teach classes and maintain control – there was a clear culture of autonomy.

By comparison, there was no such unanimity in thinking about *what* teachers should teach. Here it was possible to find an epistemological distinction between teachers who saw themselves as *specialists* and those who saw themselves as *experts*. Specialist teachers saw themselves as subject teachers, with a narrowly defined set of responsibilities. They tended to come from mathematics and science backgrounds, and were able to define the measures of satisfactory teaching in largely quantitative terms – numbers of children passing tests. The pedagogy tended to be directive, as children were seen as having to master a set body of knowledge. As specialists, they knew that there would be occasions when they would have to teach subjects which were not their specialism, and when this occurred they were happy to accept – sometimes, indeed, actively sought – direction from the specialists in that field, concerning both content and method. Equally, as specialists they expected to be able to direct non-specialists when they were teaching in their specialist area.

By comparison, expert teachers did not recognise the authority of others to direct them in their classroom practice. Instead of being specialist physicists or chemists who taught children for a living, they were teachers of children whose academic background was in a particular subject. This view was especially common among the English teachers interviewed. While they could recognise that colleagues within the department might have greater knowledge of a particular author, or be especially talented at teaching poetry, they would not acknowledge – and rarely claimed – any authority to *direct* another teacher. What did exist among the most open departments was a willingness to ask for *advice* which could then be considered, accepted or rejected. The stimulus for this had been the introduction of GCSE some two years before, which had placed all teachers together into a position in which none had expertise to offer. It was therefore legitimate to ask for advice, since all that could be offered were suggestions. The consequence was a greater sense of openness.

This point serves to demonstrate a key argument of Schein (1983), that cultures are the means by which individuals cope collectively with uncertainty. Teachers rejected the idea of discussing problems in the staffroom, because to do so was a sign of failure. Failure had to be hidden, and the way to do this was to claim autonomy and discretion. Where teachers could rest their claim to success on specialist knowledge, or acknowledge together that they were facing a totally unknown situation in which everyone's ideas might be helpful, some collaboration, sharing or direction became acceptable. Thus the nature of the knowledge upon which the culture or subculture was built was important for defining the informal norms of acceptable behaviour.

Activity 4.3

This last section has been quite complex, and it might be helpful at this stage to see if you can apply the argument to your own school. You could regard it as a test of the discussion and the categories employed. For secondary schools, you should examine your own subject department. For primary schools, it might be possible to think about the staff as a whole, but if there are more than about six teachers it might be easier to look at your colleagues working in the key stage area where you are currently teaching. In both cases, it might also be interesting to compare the attitudes of those immediate colleagues with the position of the teacher in charge of overseeing special needs provision should that be a different area. Remember that you are thinking about:

- the view of their role – specialist or expert;
- the degree of classroom autonomy they believe they should receive;
- the kind of knowledge that underpins these positions.

CULTURES OF SCHOOLING 3: OPENNESS OR PRIVACY?

The last paragraph has raised another crucial dimension to consider when thinking about school culture. Alongside the views which can be identified of the character of the teaching task, and the knowledge base upon which it is established, we have also to consider the assumptions which underpin the relationship which teachers have with their children and with one another.

Nias (1992) has suggested that teachers live a continuous paradox. Their primary concern is to establish and retain control which implies a strong sense of autonomy and discretion to do what they think is correct. However, many teachers are also very authority-dependent, happy to be told what to do and to get on with it. This willingness she identifies to get on with what they are told to do may be more apparent than real. In Scotland, Bell and Sigsworth (1990) found evidence that conformity to policy requirements was more a question of lip service than practical activity: in the classroom, teachers got on with doing things their way. Lieberman and Miller (1984) commented that this was common in the USA, both at primary and at secondary levels. The two quotations from teachers talking which they used most tellingly to make this point were the statements,

> It is safer to be private. There is some safety in the tradition, even though it keeps you lonely.

and

> I made a personal decision. I know a lot of teachers have done the same thing. You seal off the room and you deal with the students. You say, 'you and me and let's see what we can do alone.'
> (Lieberman and Miller, 1984, p. 9)

Bennett (1981) suggested that this privacy created a particular way of operating when taking decisions about the curriculum and teaching. Teachers would bring to any discussion a set of personal goals or wishes which they would seek to achieve, and another, equally important set which they were not prepared to concede. They would also bring a set of what he called, echoing sixteenth-century Anglican clerics, *adiaphora* – things indifferent, which could be conceded or sought depending on how the discussion went: negotiating points, if you like. A decision which did not achieve the desired changes would be accepted, with the mental reservation that the battle would be fought again another day, while one which challenged the reserved ground would be marginalised or ignored. It should be noted that this analysis was offered long before the national curriculum and DfE pronouncements on required teaching approaches were part of the teachers' world in England and Wales, but Scotland and the USA both have long traditions of mandated curriculum policies which teachers still appear to resist in the privacy of their classroom practice.

A widely cited reason for this emphasis on privacy, as suggested above, is that teachers are worried about appearing to be failures. Fullan and Hargreaves (1992) suggest that it is the main reason why teachers are unenthusiastic about collaborative approaches to teaching and innovation, while Smylie (1990) argues that it generates not only methodological conservatism but also another aspect of school cultures: a lack of ambition among many teachers. Bennett (1991) suggests that the fear of failure is created by the fact that most teachers are themselves successes within the educational system they staff: that success gives them legitimacy within it. For the same reason, many teachers are more willing than academics and administrators to accept the high priority placed upon GCSE performance when judging schools: it is their own academic success which gives them legitimacy in their jobs, and to deny the importance of academic success is to deny the foundation of their own position.

REVIEW

This discussion of elements which influence the culture of individual schools and shape individual teachers' responses to the demands they face has allowed us to identify some of the factors which individual middle managers will need to take into account when carrying out their duties. In Chapter 3 we examined the functions which they have to perform and the roles which they might take in carrying them out. We also explored some of the relationships between organisational culture and organisational form. We can now examine some of the views of how management and organisation fit together to shape how managers can do their jobs. In doing so, we will draw heavily on two writers. Bush (1989; 1995) has developed a widely quoted typology of educational management theories, and Hales (1993) has linked together the organisation of work within an institution and the approach which managers can take to their work.

WHAT THEORIES OF EDUCATIONAL MANAGEMENT HAVE TO COVER

A theory of educational management should be able to help us to analyse what managers in educational establishments do and how they do it. It can be *normative*, in that it puts forward statements about how the job *ought to be* done, or it can be *analytical*, offering understandings of how it *is* done. In addition, it needs to explain satisfactorily what influences and restricts the ability of a manager to act in a particular setting.

In the preceding chapters we have identified a number of factors which a theory has to take into account. These are:

- The *functions* which have to be discharged by a manager. As Table 3.1 demonstrated, these include planning, organising, commanding or directing, co-ordinating, controlling, evaluating performance, budgeting or resourcing, motivating, and setting an example.
- The *roles* through which these functions may be discharged. These may include interpersonal roles such as figurehead, leader and liaison, informational roles such as monitor, disseminator and spokesperson, and decision roles such as entrepreneur, resource allocator and negotiator.
- The *culture* of the organisation in which the manager is working, and the extent to which that culture is part of the wider culture of the work done in the organisation, or is unique to it.
- The *form of the organisation*, which may be related to its culture. This may involve forms of centralisation, such as power or role cultures, or simple or machine bureaucracies, or more decentralised organisations such as task or person cultures, or professional bureaucracies or divisionalised forms of organisation.
- The assumptions, values and 'theories in use' which collectively make up

the *personal assumptive worlds* which guide individual practice within the organisation. In particular, a theory of educational management must take account of our view of the teacher and the consequences that has for our view of what is a proper relationship between 'manager' and 'teacher'.

One issue which we have not examined in detail, although we have touched on it several times, is the basis upon which a manager is able to influence the actions of others. This is an important question, because it has a major impact on the individual manager's assumptive world. One who believes in the right to coerce colleagues is likely to act differently from one who believes that actions must rest on consensus – as the example of the school journey in Chapter 1 demonstrated.

Mintzberg (1990) argued for the basis of influence being formal authority and status: a manager is given authority by virtue of their position within the organisation. It is, in other words, delegated by those in more senior positions. In the different views of teaching proposed by Wise *et al.* (1984), the right to influence could come from positional authority if teaching was seen as labour or craft work, but be derived from personal professional competence and status if it was to be exercised over professional- or artist-teachers. However, Hales (1993) offers an alternative: the ability to influence, he argues, derives from a power relationship between the manager and the managed, which incorporates questions of formal or professional authority.

POWER AS A BASIS FOR MANAGERIAL ACTION

Hales suggests that power is a *resource,* which is deployed in an attempt to influence another's actions. It derives from possessing something which the other person lacks. This may be sheer physical strength, control over economic or financial resources, or knowledge, or may be 'normative power' – influential personal beliefs or values. Individual managers may possess these power resources by virtue of the positions they hold, or as a result of their personal characteristics. Power may be exercised overtly or covertly, and the overt exercise can be direct or through some kind of threat. In addition, it can be positive through the application of power resources, or negative, through withholding them. Hales offers examples of each in Table 4.2.

Some of these forms of power resources will be accepted as legitimate by those over whom they are exercised, and the result will be compliance. Normative resources will usually fall into this category. Others will be resisted because they are not seen as legitimate: physical resources will usually be seen as non-legitimate, but difficult to resist overtly. The others may be seen as either legitimate or non-legitimate. What is important is that it is those whom the manager seeks to influence who have to accept the exercise of power as legitimate, not those in senior positions. Thus 'authority' becomes the exercise of power resources which are seen as legitimate by those over whom they are being exercised. This can be a problem, for it has to be accepted by every

Table 4.2 Examples of the exercise of power

	Physical power	Economic power	Knowledge power	Normative power
Overt influence				
Direct/positive	Apply force/ restraint	Provide material rewards	Instruction/ persuasion/rules	Provide meanings (ideologies), 'affects'* or moral persuasion
Direct/negative	Withhold force/ restraint	Withhold material rewards	Withhold instruction/absence of rules	Fail to provide ideology, affects, or moral guidance
Threatened/ positive	Threaten force/ restraint	Promise material rewards	Suggestion	Suggest meanings/ promise affects
Threatened/ negative	Promise absence of force/restraint	Threaten to withhold material rewards	Threaten to withhold information	Threaten to withhold affects
Covert influence				
Positive	Implied threat of force (menace)	Implied promise of material rewards	Unwritten rules/ accepted practices	Taken-for-granted values/moral obligation
Negative	Implied promise of absence of restraint	Implied threat to withhold material rewards	Absence of unwritten rules/ accepted practices	Absence of taken-for-granted values or moral obligations

* For example, 'do it to please me'.

individual whose actions the manager seeks to influence. Thus the question of legitimacy is a crucial element of every individual's assumptive world, and may be interpreted quite differently by different people. Once again, this has implications for the culture of the organisation and subcultures within it. For example, is the 'specialist' teacher likely to accept as legitimate the same power resources as those acknowledged by the 'expert'? Or the professional-teacher the same power resources as the craft-teacher?

The degree to which the exercise of power resources is seen as legitimate is not the only factor in determining whether it will be successful. If it takes a non-legitimate form, such as a threat of physical punishment, then the result might be what Hales calls 'alienative compliance', in which the instruction or direction is carried out but the relationship between manager and managed is soured. However, if the person being threatened is strong enough, or, in Hales' terms, possesses sufficient resources of their own, then the result may be non-compliance. This raises a very important point for managers: they are dependent on the actions of those they manage for success, just as much as those they manage may be dependent on them for things like guidance, direction and resources. The relationship between the manager and the managed is therefore an *exchange* relationship, in which the successful exercise of managerial influence depends upon an imbalance of resources in their favour. This is why normative power resources – the exercise of moral persuasion or suggestion – is likely to be important, but also why economic and knowledge resources, in the shape of money, rewards, knowledge of the rules and procedures or high levels of competence within the subject, are likely to be significant factors in developing a stronger certainty of compliance. Managers frequently work to create dependency relationships among others (Kotter 1977).

This might be taken to imply that management is ultimately a matter of coercion. This is not so, for coercion will not gain commitment and will only survive for as long as there is an imbalance of resources. Hence in Handy's (1985) power culture there is often a rapid turnover of 'middle managers', since if they become too knowledgeable they may challenge the position of the person at the centre of the web. Consequently, they are often fired before they become too good at their jobs, creating an unstable and high-stress working environment.

Instead of operating by coercion, ultimately a manager must operate by consent. Mintzberg (1979) sees the simple (power) cultural form as maturing into a machine bureaucracy (a role culture) because the nature of the dependency relationship changes. Managers accept their individual responsibilities within a broader system. However, the imbalance of resources remains. Middle managers develop limited areas of responsibility and functional specialisms, while senior managers keep the overall view. Nonetheless, the acceptance of defined roles and responsibilities, and established procedures for completing tasks, demonstrates a fundamental consent to the management process.

It also reveals another important aspect of management which differentiates it from ownership, which is often what is to be found at the centre of the web in the power culture. Management seeks to depersonalise the power resources, so that they are seen to derive from the office rather than the person. However, it is very difficult to do this when thinking about normative power resources, and also hard to distinguish the exercise of economic or knowledge resources by the individual who holds the office from the person. Nevertheless, much management writing attempts to do this – Mintzberg (1990) was concerned to do so and it is particularly a feature of the first of the theories of management we shall look at.

EVALUATING THEORIES OF EDUCATIONAL MANAGEMENT

Armed with these considerations, we can evaluate the effectiveness of educational management theories as a guide to management practice. Theories, as has been said already, can be offered as all-embracing, universal constructs to be applied in every setting, or as perspectives to be drawn on as appropriate. The latter approach further undermines the 'unique' argument about education, and in line with that earlier claim the rest of the chapter examines a variety of different perspectives from which to analyse educational management practice. It uses the classification of theories developed by Tony

Bush (1989, 1995), who proposes that we can distinguish five distinct perspectives: bureaucratic, collegial, political, subjective, and ambiguity.

THE BUREAUCRATIC PERSPECTIVE

Those who see schools as bureaucracies are concerned to create a rational structure for organising work and managing the activities of those who do it. Bureaucracy is a much-maligned word, but as a managerial form and perspective it continues to be popular in both private and public sector organisations.

Bureaucracies have the following characteristics:

- A clear logic is perceived to exist between the goals of the organisation and the actions which must be taken to achieve them. They are therefore believed to be rational organisations.
- Responsibilities and duties are clearly laid down and distinguished. This leads to a high degree of specialisation among the workforce.
- Because of this specialisation, there is a strong centralisation of decision-making at the most senior levels of the organisation, so that all the disparate specialisms work in harmony.
- Consequently, there are clear rules of procedure laid down for the specialists to follow, which are laid down centrally.
- There is a hierarchy of staff to transmit and enforce these rules. Since a primary function of more senior posts in the hierarchy is to supervise the work of less senior postholders, hierarchies are typically pyramidal in form.
- There are clear lines of accountability drawn between the different levels in the hierarchy.
- An individual's accountability is as a holder of an office, and to a holder of another office, and not between individuals.
- The hierarchical structure of differentiated specialists encourages vertical communication through the system rather than direct horizontal communication between specialists.

All of these characteristics make for a system in which control of actions is pervasive, flexibility is limited and individuality unacceptable. Hales (1993) comments that management action in a bureaucracy rests on a faith in rationality in which problems call forth more regulations, nothing is left to chance, and innovation is almost impossible. It is a characterisation of Handy's (1993) 'role culture', or Mintzberg's (1979) 'machine bureaucracy', discussed in Chapter 3. It also fits comfortably with the systems model outlined there.

A bureaucracy is also expected to be a unified institution, since everyone is working to the same set of rules. These rules will have been established in order to achieve certain objectives or goals, which will have been accepted by the postholders within the system, as part of their acceptance of the rules and procedures which govern their behaviour and the authority which derives from the posts they hold. Bureaucratic management is therefore concerned with ensuring that people carry out the rules in order to achieve the goals which have been laid down, with putting right problems as they arise, and with informing the goal-setters of problems which cannot be dealt with. It is an objective, detached and intellectual process which rests on an assumption of consensus about the goals being pursued, the means being followed, and the distribution of power resources within the organisation.

In key respects, the bureaucratic model has much to offer secondary schools, although its value for primary schools may be more limited. Secondary schools have to organise the work of specialists. They need to operate according to rules in order to move large numbers of children from one specialist to another – what Lieberman and Miller (1984) call 'batch processing' – and to ensure that information about individual pupils and classes is collated and passed to all those who need to know it. All schools need to ensure that there is continuity and consistency of practice in the children's learning experiences, and the national curriculum increases the pressure for uniformity of practice. In addition, Hales (1993) points out the following advantages in a well-managed bureaucracy:

- delegated decision-making within central overall control;
- swift and consistent central decisions, based on wide feedback;
- hierarchical structures allow for succession planning – identifying future senior staff and 'grooming' them for promotion – and allows loyalty to be rewarded;
- impersonal adherence to the rules avoids quirky decisions and actions resting on personal preferences.

Bureaucratic middle managers are concerned to ensure that procedures are followed in order to complete the work satisfactorily. They pass information on about requirements and progress, and ensure that the values of the organisation are understood and shared. They have an important part to play in inducting new staff into the norms of the organisation. As possessors of economic and knowledge resources, they can gain the respect and support of their subordinates and so bring about compliance. The similarities between this set of responsibilities and those involved in communicating the vision of the leadership to others, outlined in Chapter 2 as a key responsibility of 'middle management', are striking.

However, there are problems in bureaucratic approaches. Those taking decisions at the centre can become isolated from the place where the core work is done, and unaware of what it is like. The information passed up to them can be out-of-date, or get distorted or 'sanitised' if it is thought likely to be unpopular, while downward-flowing information may get distorted by managers who either misunderstand it or for some reason do not subscribe to the organisation's values and are pursuing personal goals rather than those of the organisation. Because they originate from sources remote from the action, rules may be unworkable or irrelevant, or seen as such, and so get bent or ignored, leading to problems for managers. Alternatively, they may result in alienative compliance, as the rules are followed but generate staff hostility towards management and the regulations they produce. Further, strict adherence to the rules may become an excuse for inaction or 'passing the buck'. The unsuccessful manager who does not develop a career may become alienated or demotivated, and there is plenty of room for the development of rivalries between units and departments. This gives rise to micropolitical activity, which we discuss below. Before we do so, however, we should examine the characteristics of a popular view of management which is often put forward as the professional alternative to bureaucracies: collegiality.

Activity 4.4

'Bureaucracy' is often used to describe a structure rather than a theory of management, and also as a term of abuse! To test the theory, consider this question. If your school was a 'proper', fully-functioning bureaucracy, how would a decision be taken and implemented to introduce a new format for pupil reports to parents?

I give my answer in the appendix, but try it for yourself first!

THE COLLEGIAL PERSPECTIVE

The key characteristics of collegiality as a means of organising and managing work are as follows:

- People work as autonomous individuals, with a minimum of rules or guidance from above.
- Individuals influence others on the basis of expertise and knowledge instead of position.
- Because they are autonomous, they have to consent to the minimum rules which exist.
- There is a common understanding among the autonomous individuals of the nature of their work, and the fields of responsibility of each person, which rest on shared fundamental values. Thus autonomous individuals share common goals and purposes which can be taken to be the goals and purposes of the organisation in which they work.
- The ultimate authority for taking decisions rests with the autonomous individuals working as a collectivity, and not at some central or senior point within a hierarchy or network.
- Decisions have to be taken democratically by that collective of individuals, because only in this way can their commitment to and acceptance of a decision be guaranteed.
- Because each individual is autonomous and working under a minimum of regulation, the only basis on which decisions can be taken is rational debate. Collegial organisations are therefore rational organisations.

Like bureaucracies, then, collegial organisations rest on a fundamental assumption of consent. However, whereas the consent of members of a bureaucracy derives from their accepting membership of the organisation and abiding by the rules and procedures laid down by senior staff, collegial consent is achieved by the shared understanding of the needs of the work and the active participation in making all the decisions which relate to each individual.

In a collegium, 'management' does not exist. Instead, the autonomous worker is supported by administrators, who provide and organise the facilities and resources necessary to enable the work to be carried out. In this sense, a collegium matches with Wise *et al.*'s (1984) idea of the teacher-professional.

Collegiality matches most closely with Handy's (1993) person culture, which he suggests can only exist in small organisations, and it is certainly the case that larger organisations which claim to run on collegial principles are often burdened with cumbersome decision-making processes. Committees, subcommittees and executive committees, all answerable to an assembly of members who can overturn their decisions and recommendations, can all be as slow-moving as a bureaucratic referral system. However, many decisions which bureaucratic systems would need to take at senior levels because of their highly rule-bound nature would be taken by individuals in a collegium. Further, although the process is slow, it produces deep levels of commitment to the decision and its implementation because it is consensual and, in theory at least, rational.

The possibility of a structure of committees, and the existence of administrative support, makes it possible to see Mintzberg's 'professional bureaucracy' as an organisational and cultural form for collegial management. This kind of culture strengthens the separation of administration from the primary work task, and reduces the extent to which the autonomous professionals undertake managerial responsibility. Whereas in a bureaucracy every aspect of work is directed, in a professional bureaucracy procedural controls would be restricted to administrative tasks such as raising purchase orders, and these are done by administrators rather than professionals. The only professional duties which would be regulated in this way would be activities like making staff appointments, where legal procedures have to be followed, or activities which the staff had agreed collectively should be subject to rules. Agreeing school journeys, or communications with parents, might be examples of this.

The manager in a fully-fledged collegial organisation does not exist. Instead, individuals will accept administrative responsibilities. However, in a committee-structured system, there is room for more senior professionals, or those who are appointed by their colleagues, to become involved in decision-making. The dimensions of management concerned with control and direction, however, are absent, and co-ordination is typically an administrative responsibility.

Activity 4.5
It would be a good idea to repeat Activity 4.4 now, but in a fully-fledged collegial school rather than a 'pure' bureaucratic organisation. Indeed, it is also suggested that you repeat it at the end of each of the next three sections, analysing the way decisions would be taken in a school operating within that theoretical perspective. I will not comment on those, but do respond in the appendix to this activity.

Because collegiality depends on a set of shared values, it cannot, by definition, be imposed, but has to grow as a set of values which can then be transformed into a set of procedures. Thus creating a collegial organisation is complex and difficult, requiring vision and leadership, the communication of values and their acceptance by the teachers involved. Nias, Southworth and Yeomans (1989) explored the development of collegiality and what they referred to as a culture of collaboration in five primary schools, and recognised both the crucial role of the headteacher in bringing it about and the need to work gently to bring it about through converting the teachers' view of 'normal' behaviour. When teachers share their classroom concerns they will also share wider decisions, and acknowledge the constraints they create.

A fully collegial view of educational management, then, has to marry the autonomous and egalitarian view of staff with external obligations and accountability and a hierarchical career structure. It has also to take account of the extent to which the fundamental work of the school depends on rules and procedures in order to function. Typically, collegial-committee systems operate with the professional staff who take senior managerial responsibilities doing so for a short period of time only. The consequence of this tension is that staff who are in permanent senior positions often talk of collegiality when they mean participation by less senior staff in a decision-making process which leaves the final responsibility at the top of a hierarchy. Hargreaves (1992) refers to this as 'contrived collegiality'.

It is possible to find examples of collegiality within individual departments or other sections of apparently bureaucratic organisations, but these then become subcultural characteristics, and possibly counter-cultural in that the assumptions of collegiality – authority of expertise, consensus and shared values – may stand at odds with the wider values of the formal organisation as expressed in its official decision-making structures and allocation of roles and responsibilities, and the declared attitudes of the senior staff. This possibility returns us to the prospect of micropolitical activity within the organisation, which removes at a stroke the consensual foundations of both bureaucracy and collegiality.

THE MICROPOLITICAL PERSPECTIVE

Micropolitical views of management (political models) make the following assumptions:

- There is no consensus among the staff in an organisation over its goals or ideology.
- Therefore the starting-point of analysing how organisations operate and thinking about the manager's role must be individuals rather than the organisation as a whole.
- How power resources, especially knowledge and normative resources, are distributed among staff is not clear, since the goals and ideology of the

organisation are not universally agreed. Staff who favour the organisation's formal goals will allow more influence to those whose knowledge supports their realisation than they will to colleagues whose knowledge appears to favour alternative goals.

- In the absence of consensus, individuals pursue individual goals and seek ways of improving their chances of achieving them. Coalitions of like-minded staff therefore develop as interest-groups: individuals form groups, whose behaviour is the basis of political activity.

- Because goals are not shared and different power resources are recognised as valid by individuals and interest groups, conflict over what is proper action in any situation is normal.

- Interest groups seek to increase their power resources, especially normative resources which are usually seen as legitimate by colleagues, but also economic resources which can increase others' dependency upon them.

- Interest groups may rest upon formal structural subunits, such as subject departments in secondary schools, on informal subunits created by structural decisions, such as a group of teachers who have taught mainly in a lower school annexe over many years, or on informal groupings, such as shared political beliefs.

- Interest groups may be secure and apparently permanent or temporary alliances for particular issues. The strongest and most enduring interest groups are those which are brought together by common ideological and economic bonds.

- The actions of individuals and groups in pursuit of their goals are governed by informal rules and norms which lay down the limits of acceptable behaviour in bargaining and negotiation.

- Decisions which result from the bargaining and negotiation process are only accepted to the extent that they are seen as matching individual interests or open to amendment at a later date.

The fundamental assumption behind the micropolitical perspective, then, is one of conflict as a normal and everyday activity which has to be managed actively. It is therefore incompatible with the principles of collegiality or bureaucracy. However, it is quite at home within bureaucratic or collegial *structures*, since these can coexist with a lack of the consensus they require if they are to operate with maximum effectiveness. The result is merely a less effective organisation! Political managers seek to promote one set of interests over others at any particular time, in pursuit of the particular needs or wishes of the interest groups to which they belong. The needs of the subunits for which they are responsible are the primary focus of such management activity, for success in promoting their area of responsibility is the route to promotion.

Political management styles can also coexist with collegial or bureaucratic styles. While managers may operate in a highly political manner in the wider school setting, seeking to increase the power resources at their disposal and so to increase the influence they can have on decisions on behalf of their unit of responsibility, within that unit they might operate in bureaucratic or collegial manner, laying down clear rules of procedure or ensuring a high degree of autonomy among colleagues within agreed minimal controls. This will only be possible, of course, if there is a clear consensus among the staff within their area of responsibility on the nature of teaching, methods, purposes, and epistemology.

Political views of school management are particularly prevalent in analyses of secondary schools, where the interest-groups are often formally defined. Subject departments have to compete for resources, for a place on the timetable, and for satisfactory staffing by specialists rather than depending on teachers whose main subject specialism (and therefore, by implication, loyalty) is in another department. Pursuit and protection of those interests is seen as the key driving force behind teacher action within the school: the sole motivation of political actors is some kind of 'profit'. The political view recognises the different epistemological bases of the departments and their varying statuses – maths and science departments may be able to claim disproportionately more resources than music or CDT, while European Studies is discontinued altogether – and therefore argues that we can expect to find the weaker subunits forming alliances with stronger ones in order to increase their opportunities to gain resources or influence policy decisions.

Political models of management also see the informal subcultures as being important. They see power and influence as being more significant than formal authority in affecting attitudes and decisions. Further, they recognise that a decision to do something is not the same thing as having it happen, and that all kinds of opportunities exist to block the implementation of policy decisions, even when these decisions appear to have the democratic approval of the staff. Thus ideological disputes are to be expected within political schools, whereas collegial schools will not be hampered by such activities. Further, because political models see the decision-making and implementation process as one which takes place across a variety of arenas – departmental meeting, faculty meeting, senior management meeting, staff meeting, and so on – it is possible for influence to be exercised in a variety of ways and at a variety of points of the process. Individuals might be active within individual meetings, or active in lobbying colleagues privately before a meeting takes place. Thus a decision at one level might not resolve the issue because unsuccessful individuals or groups can seize or create opportunities to bring the matter up again.

Although the starting-point for analysis within the political perspective is individual action rather than the whole organisation, it shifts the focus of management's attention not to individuals so much as to groups. Instead of trying to fuse the different individuals into a coherent and unified whole, managers need to cope with a multiplicity of group interests and establish a *modus vivendi* between them. With our move to the next perspective, we change our emphasis again, from a focus on groups to a focus on individuals.

THE SUBJECTIVE PERSPECTIVE

This perspective is less well developed than the others outlined here, but is included because it is popular among some writers on school management. It derives largely from the work of Greenfield (e.g. Greenfield and Ribbins 1993). Its key characteristics are:

- Organisations have no objective existence independent of their members.
- Organisational goals do not exist: only individual people can have goals. What are usually called organisational goals are the personal goals of powerful individuals within the organisation.
- Organisational structures exist as the interaction of individuals rather than as formalised responsibility relationships. It is what people do that matters, not who they are supposed to be. Therefore, changing the formal structure will only change practice if the attitudes of the people whose jobs are represented in the organisation chart also change.
- Because of this, the key factor to consider is what meanings individuals attach to events rather than the events themselves, and these may vary about the same event from person to person. Therefore, there might be competing realities in schools, rather than an objective 'truth'. For example, Best *et al.* (1981, 1983) found five competing perspectives on a school's pastoral care policy among the school staff, each of which generated a different perception of what teachers ought to do in pastoral care roles, their responsibility to others, and the management roles of those with responsibility for pastoral care in the school.

The subjective perspective relates strongly to the idea of individual assumptive worlds with which this chapter began. By ensuring attention is paid to the individuals in the organisation and the meanings they attach to events, it enables the manager to be more sensitive to individual concerns. It creates a moral imperative and places normative power resources at the heart of one person's ability to influence another. However, it does not address the question of whether any individual has the right to exercise that influence: that is addressed normatively through bureaucratic and collegial perspectives, and pragmatically through the political perspective. It focuses on quite a different set of concerns from the other perspectives reviewed so far. The bureaucratic perspective emphasises one's managerial obligation to the goals and values of senior staff, while the collegial perspective stresses one's managerial responsibility to facilitate the professional work of autonomous individuals in as decentralised a system as possible. The political perspective stresses one's obligation to oneself to pursue personal goals through a process of bargaining and conflict. The subjective perspective provides a guiding principle in action by offering a way of thinking about the relationships between individuals who work in the same school, and how they influence one another and the perception each one has of the 'organisation' which they create.

AMBIGUITY PERSPECTIVES

As befits the name, there is more than one formulation of the 'ambiguity' view of schools. However, we can identify the following key characteristics within them:

- Our primary focus returns from the individual in the organisation to the organisation as a whole.
- Educational organisations are non-rational in that there is no incontrovertible proof of a relationship between what a school does (its 'technology') and the achievement of its goals. Decisions to do 'X' in order to achieve 'Y' therefore rest ultimately on faith, not rational thought.
- The relationship between the actions of one sub-unit of a school and the others is often problematic, as is the extent to which they make up a coherent set of activities for the school as a whole.
- The goals of schools are themselves subject to debate, and those formally declared for a school are likely to be rejected by some or all of its staff.
- Participation in decision-making activity is fluid, in that some people do not get involved at all, others are involved all the time, but many only get involved when the issue being decided has direct relevance to their personal work and when it is important enough to take precedence over other activities.
- Problems do not get solved by a rational process of identifying a difficulty, searching for alternatives and choosing a solution. Instead, a range of problems, possible choices and solutions exist simultaneously in individual perceptions and both private and public debate, and which ones get acknowledged and chosen depends on who is participating in the decision-making process at the time.
- Because individuals and groups often have particular goals of their own, and 'pet solutions' which they wish to see implemented, the solutions which are finally decided upon may bear little or no relation to the problem originally brought up as needing attention.

The degree to which problems, choices and solutions are entirely decoupled from each other is a matter for debate between writers using this perspective. Its originators, Cohen and March (1974), saw them as entirely decoupled: participants in decision-making dump problems, choices and solutions in a 'garbage can' from which they are drawn out depending on who is participating at the time and how important they consider a particular issue to be. If relevant specialists are not available or choose not to take part, the solution adopted may not be the most suitable, and if powerful or articulate individuals or groups have pushed 'pet solutions' there may be no relationship at all between the actions decided on and the problem they are intended to deal with.

Against this, Weick (1976) has suggested that problems, choices and solutions are 'loosely coupled' together, in that each event is connected to others, but preserves its own identity. Further, individual parts of a school – classrooms, departments/faculties, or pastoral units – are themselves only loosely coupled to one another. For example, discipline problems concerning a particular child may affect a large number of teachers in different subjects, and the work not just of the child in question but of most of the children in the classes he or she attends. The discipline problems of each teacher are therefore coupled together, but each teacher can, if necessary, find an independent solution to the problem. These solutions may conflict with each other, so that the child gets conflicting messages about what is expected, and the teachers who are less successful in coping with the problem find the discipline problem is increased. If the school is one in which discipline issues are, to begin with, dealt with by departments rather than within the pastoral system, and the culture of the teaching staff is one which finds it difficult to acknowledge 'failure', then it is likely that each subject department will sort out its own solution. Loose coupling is a way in which this separation of a problem into many individual, apparently disconnected parts, can be coped with analytically. It creates a view of the school as an organisation, and allows the manager to begin to frame a way of dealing with a perceived problem.

Bush (1990) points out that a view of schools as loosely coupled also provides a means of containing potentially damaging or destabilising problems. A weak element in the system can to some extent be sealed off from the others so that it does not create too many problems elsewhere. However, loose coupling does not mean uncoupling: the example above demonstrates that there will still be consequences needing attention.

Through its emphasis on the non-rational nature of much organisational activity, and the problematic nature of much staff involvement and participation, the ambiguity perspective raises important concerns which a manager must address. However, the way in which they are addressed will in itself depend on the individual manager's assumptive world. For example, if a head of department believes that collegial decision-making should be the norm within the department, then it will be necessary to address both the feelings and beliefs of those who never attend and of those who participate some of the time. The reasons for their actions (or inaction) may be different. On the other hand, someone who favours laying down bureaucratic-style rules and procedures will have to approach the individual teacher in the knowledge that their private classrooms are only loosely connected to the others unless actions can be taken to open them up.

Management in non-rational, ambiguous organisations is hard to categorise and analyse. Mintzberg's (1990) characterisation is probably the most helpful.

But the fact that a school may be most effectively analysed from an ambiguity perspective does not remove any management function from the manager's responsibility. Planning, co-ordinating, budgeting, commanding and controlling remain legitimate demands for senior management to place upon middle managers. What is affected is not what is done, but how it can be done, and one is drawn back to the view of management as involving interpersonal, informational and decisional roles which allow the manager to cope with the complexity and confusion which is likely to be the result. However, non-rational management in a non-rational world is not the same as irrational management. Non-rational managers still have goals, which may be their own or those laid down for the organisation. They look for ways of pursuing and achieving those goals. What is non-rational, because it rests ultimately on faith rather than fact, is the connection between the actions they take and those goals being achieved.

WHICH PERSPECTIVE IS BEST?

The short answer is, it depends! Bush (1990, 1993) emphasises repeatedly that the theories are not mutually exclusive but are 'heuristics', devices for analysing the organisation in which you work in order to understand a particular situation. However, it is important to connect each of these to your personal assumptive world. Certain perspectives will have made more sense to you than others, because they will have chimed with your view of your school, or with your experience of other schools. You may have found yourself thinking that one explained what you experienced in your last school, while another is a better characterisation of what is going on where you work now. What you have to do as a manager is to marry up your understanding of how your current school operates in practice with what you believe, as a manager and a teacher, you ought to be doing.

Each perspective emphasises different aspects of how people are expected to act in schools, and work on different assumptions. A summary of the different perspectives and their characteristics is given in Table 4.3

It has been implied several times in this chapter that the bureaucratic model has much to offer secondary schools, but that it has problems that give rise to political activity. We shall look in more detail at its applicability in Chapter 7. But which model of organisation and management is most appropriate to primary schools? We turn to consider this question in Chapters 5 and 6.

Table 4.3 Summary of characteristics of different perspectives on educational management

	Assumptions about nature of organisation	Assumptions about individual involvement	Nature of individual's relation to organisation	Concept of individual role	Perceived source of influence and accountability	Power resources acknowledged and available	Location of decision-making	Nature of middle management role/function	Degree of planning possible or acknowledged	Nature of decision-making
Bureaucratic	Rational	Consensual / Normative/moral commitment / Total	Rule bound / Directed	Specialist / Clearly specified duties	Office / Impersonal	Knowledge / Economic / Normative	Centralised, but delegated with overall control	Control / Command / Monitor / Resource / Report	Long-term, by senior staff	Rational consideration of information against objectives
Collegial	Rational	Consensual / Normative/moral commitment / Total	Autonomous within agreed minimum constraints	Autonomous Professional / Consensual understanding of responsibilities but not detailed application	Professional competence and obligation	Knowledge / Normative	Decentralised, or by democratic central body	Facilitate / Co-ordinate / Resource / Disseminate	Can be long-term, by a central body	Rational, democratic debate
Micro-political	Rational	Conflictual / Calculative and limited / Informal norms	Instrumental pursuit of personal goals within the organisational setting	Self-interested / Degree of autonomy/specification dependent on context	Variable depending on issue and goal-congruence	All	Depends on who involved and structure of organisation	Negotiator / Resource / Leader / Control	Problematic: degree of political control influences extent of planning	Bargaining and negotiation. Never finalised: always open to renegotiation

and micro-political skill

Subjectivist	Organisation is a collection of individuals	Dependent on invividual perception and personal commitment	All	Individual	Spokesperson / Disturbance handler / Entrepreneur / Leader / Liaison / Facilitate / Support / Disseminate / Disturbance-handler	Problematic	Individual negotiation and commitment
Ambiguity	Non-rational	Problematic and issue-dependent	All	Variable: issue- and structure-dependent	Any of all	Problematic due to non-rational nature of decision-making	Non-rational: 'garbage can'

5

Middle Management and the Primary School

CAN PRIMARY SCHOOLS HAVE MIDDLE MANAGERS?

Three questions guide this discussion of which models of organisation and management are most appropriate for primary schools. Who are 'middle managers' in primary schools? What are they expected to do? How do they interpret their role and responsibilities? But one prior question is, can primary schools have middle managers at all? In Chapter 1 we quoted one headteacher as declaring that he did not find the term 'acceptable'. Before we examine these questions, I suggest you do Activity 5.1.

Activity 5.1
On the basis of your experience, how would you answer each of the four questions in the previous paragraph? What reasons would you offer to support your answers? The rest of the first part of this chapter addresses these questions.

Several points do indeed cast doubt on whether 'middle management' and primary schools are compatible. Three in particular are worth examining.

1. Most primary schools have ten or fewer full-time equivalent teaching staff, and under three hundred pupils. This restricts the extent to which a formal hierarchy of posts can be created. Few if any primary schools have ever awarded teachers four responsibility points or 'D' allowances, and teachers on three additional points are rarely to be found outside large urban schools. Consequently, at least until new conditions of service were imposed in 1987, only limited delegation to individual teachers occurred because of their office, and primary schools have typically been less bureaucratic than secondary schools, with far less demarcation of responsibilities.

The absence of a long hierarchy of promotions affects the nature of career expectations among primary teachers, for there would not be the sense, strong within secondary schools, that staff must move frequently to progress up a longer ladder of promotions towards senior status and headship. This influences both the candidates' expectations of the workload in promoted posts and the expectations of their colleagues of what postholders do and how they do it.

2. Primary schools are usually organised on the basis of one teacher taking responsibility for all the learning of a class of children for the whole year. This creates a far more complex web of relationships between teachers than typically exists in secondary schools, where subject teachers teach a specific subject to a large number of groups of children. The secondary school structure, in which teachers are answerable at least nominally to the head of their subject department, is not operational in a primary school. Other kinds of structures, and their associated interpersonal relationships, are needed.

Primary teachers' involvement with their pupils can become more time-consuming and all-embracing than that of secondary teachers, especially if the children are very young, since they become much more aware of the needs of a much smaller group of children. They have to balance the obligations of teaching and care more acutely than their secondary colleagues, who frequently have the support of pastoral care teams.

An important result of this is that, as Lieberman and Miller (1984) demonstrated, individual teachers can become isolated from one another unless specific attempts are made to overcome it. The classroom and its pupils can become 'their domain', separated from the rest of the school. Since very few primary teachers have any non-contact time, only the headteacher has the opportunity to overcome this insularity on a regular basis.

3. Primary schools have a majority of female staff. Whatever the desirability of the social attitudes which surround gender issues, it remains true that this has important consequences. Many will experience a career break for children. Family responsibilities are still borne largely by the mother, which may further interfere with professional career ambitions. Many women still accept the husband as the primary breadwinner and tailor their own career moves, if any, to those of their partner. When this is linked to the relative lack of a hierarchically structured career progression, the consequence is a stable nucleus of teachers in most primary schools. This can reinforce the tendencies to insularity and fragmentation just referred to, and make change extremely difficult to bring about.

All these factors have influenced thinking and writing about primary schools and their management. Most official documents prior to 1987 speak of primary schools as if they are the property of the headteacher (Alexander 1984), and even now most writing on primary school management is directed firmly at the head, even when the language is that of participatory management and the claimed focus on senior or middle management (e.g. Day, Whitaker and Johnson 1990). In this, there is a strong echo of the arguments about vision and leadership laid out in Chapter 2. But alongside this possessive streak the professional literature has always employed a rhetoric of collegiality, in which the primary school is a harmonious community of equals who take decisions together and work collectively to implement them. Such collegiality was commonly claimed by headteachers on management development courses I was involved in tutoring in the 1980s, and is well demonstrated in this extract from the further particulars of a job advertised in May 1994:

The school has a well-established policy of involving all members of staff in decision-making. There is no senior management team as the existence of such a group would be inappropriate, demeaning to those not invited to join and contrary to the school's recognition that all teachers are managers and professional development is best enhanced by giving everyone the opportunity to participate in all aspects of school management.

THE TASKS AND DUTIES OF PRIMARY SCHOOL POSTHOLDERS

What, then, distinguishes the work of postholders from colleagues who do not hold additional responsibility points or allowances? The first clear statement of what was officially expected came from HMI in the 1978 Primary Survey (DES 1978). Postholders were expected to plan schemes of work with the head, supervise their operation, advise and encourage colleagues, and assess the schemes' effectiveness; to learn to lead groups of colleagues and work in co-operation with them. This view, which stressed subject knowledge and understanding of children's learning, was refined by 1982 into the concept of the curriculum 'consultant' in first schools (DES 1982), who was portrayed as the purveyor of advice and support to colleagues. The activities listed in these official reports match with the less mechanistic views of management examined in Chapter 3, and respect classroom autonomy. Importantly, however, they also avoid the question of delegating responsibility. From these perspectives, postholders may be involved in planning and supervising the operation of schemes of work, but it is not clear that they would have any authority to seek changes in the practice of teachers whose work was thought to be out of line. Indeed, the use of the term 'consultant' can be argued explicitly to deny such authority. Consultant teachers can therefore be seen as operating as agents of the head, whose full control is sustained and to whom, alone, the individual teacher receiving the consultant's advice is accountable. It thus sustains the official rhetoric of the school as the personal field of the headteacher, and this is still retained by the widespread use of the term 'co-ordinator' in both job descriptions and much research.

The distinction between 'managers' and 'co-ordinators' or 'consultants' is important, and lies in the underlying concept of the individual's work. Co-ordinators relate to teachers as professionals or artists (Wise *et al.* 1984). They work with teachers who have high levels of autonomy and discretion in their classroom work, and must therefore work by consensus and the negotiated individual consent of each teacher. Managers may *choose* to operate in this way, but are assumed to retain some measure of control over what teachers do. Thus, in the official literature down to 1987, heads could not be co-ordinators, because individual teachers would acquire what central government saw as an unacceptable measure of autonomy and reduce the extent to which an individual head was accountable for all the work of all the teachers in the school. Individual teachers, however, could act as co-ordinators on behalf of the head. If they were to act as managers, then the head would have to delegate sufficient authority to them to enable them to carry out the management function. The implications of delegation for redistributing power resources in a small organisation are sizeable.

The conditions of service imposed by the government in 1987 to end the long-running teachers' pay dispute altered this view of the postholder's role somewhat. It required all schools to establish job descriptions for every member of staff, so that for the first time it became possible to identify more precisely what promoted posts were being awarded for. Importantly for this study, the conditions of service laid down for *main scale* teachers included the following:

> Advising and co-operating with the headteachers and other teachers . . . on the preparation and development of courses of study, teaching materials, teaching programmes, methods of teaching and assessment and pastoral arrangements . . .
>
> Co-ordinating or managing the work of other teachers.
>
> (DES 1987, Schedule 3, paras 3.1, 3.12)

This statement gave to main scale teachers the basic responsibilities often exercised in the past by postholders. Importantly, this official conditions of service order was the first occasion when anyone other than a headteacher was described in an official document as having responsibility for *managing* anything in a primary school. As far as official wisdom is concerned, then, it appears that everyone is a manager in a primary school. This would suggest that those who hold promoted positions might be 'middle managers' if they have responsibility for overseeing the management work of main grade or standard scale colleagues. Thus we find ourselves being drawn by official conditions of service towards a bureaucratic model, with control and delineation of duties as the key defining characteristics. Further, the term 'middle' management implies that there is a senior tier above them, and we must identify who occupies it – if it really exists – and what the relationship is between the tiers.

Is it true, then, that all teachers have management responsibilities and that postholders are paid for additional managerial duties of some sort? To try and find out, and to examine relationships between teachers in different levels of seniority, data were collected on the nature of promoted posts through a series of surveys conducted in each of the years 1991–1994. Schools were asked for the further particulars they were sending out to enquiries about advertised vacancies, and, if possible, to complete a short questionnaire which asked the headteacher to identify which posts in the school were seen as 'middle management' and why, along with some information about what their expectations were of the successful applicant.

In addition, a sample of promoted postholders in smaller schools was interviewed to explore their perceptions of their role and responsibilities and the influences which worked upon them. Case studies were prepared from these data and sent to other postholders in different geographical areas for comment.

The response to the requests for information was patchy, and it was very difficult to establish any significant pattern in the job descriptions, but they provide useful information about what is seen as appropriate responsibilities to merit receipt of an allowance, what is seen as 'middle management', and the ways in which those responsibilities are seen as being carried out. The next part of this chapter will summarise the survey findings.

WHAT CURRENT JOB DESCRIPTIONS AND JOB HOLDERS TELL US

1. How 'C' posts and those with three responsibility points were viewed

The small number of 'C'/3 posts whose job descriptions were received were all described as senior management in the job descriptions themselves, but some were categorised as middle management on the accompanying questionnaire. The further particulars for 'C'/3 posts always showed this senior management team to consist of the head and deputy and any 'C'/3s in the school, and made no reference to any 'B'/2 postholders, but further particulars on 'B'/2 posts sometimes described them as senior management. These were usually, but not always, in schools which did not have any posts with three responsibility points. The schools offering 'C'/3 posts were all relatively large, with over 400 pupils; all were primary schools rather than junior or infants' schools. However, there was no clear pattern among this small number of senior positions as to the duties assigned to the post, except for their being expected to meet with the head and deputy, and undertake aspects of whole-school planning and management. These responsibilities were kept vague, occasionally being covered by a statement that precise details would be agreed with the successful candidate.

2. How 'B' posts, and those with two responsibility points, were viewed

There was far less clarity here, and some conflict between the information in the job descriptions for the 'B'/2 posts and that in the questionnaires. In the latter, three-quarters of the 'B'/2 posts were defined as middle management, and all but one of the remainder were senior management. Questionnaires accompanying 'C'/3 details all called 'B'/2 posts middle management. However, in a substantial minority of cases jobs categorised as middle management in the questionnaires were defined as senior management in the accompanying job description.

It was not always clear that there was a senior/middle management distinction, since some 'B'/2 posts were seen as part of a less hierarchically expressed 'management team', with the head and deputy. This was variously stated as 'being a senior member of the curriculum team' or 'being a member of the senior team/senior management team'.

Two broad strands were identified in the 'B'/2 posts advertised. Some had whole-school responsibilities which clearly saw them as co-ordinating the work of other staff who held designated responsibilities, for example as 'co-ordinator of the subject co-ordinators'. Other school-wide responsibilities included co-ordination of assessment, and being in charge of a key stage. 'B'/2 postholders with such responsibilities were more frequently seen as members of a school-wide management team with the head and deputy, and included posts similar to those accorded 'C'/3 allowances elsewhere. Two examples were the head of an infants department in a largish primary school, who had a range of staff deployment and timetabling responsibilities, and a 'phase team' leader, who was seen as having responsibility for co-ordinating a range of curriculum co-ordinators, most of whom were operating as standard scale teachers. This last was one of the few posts which specifically asked for personal qualities like initiative, drive and flexibility, and the only post which stated that the holder would be responsible not just for planning the curriculum but also for its delivery and monitoring and for recording pupils' work. However, a number of other job descriptions made it clear that the tasks of planning, delivery, monitoring and recording were widely seen as classroom responsibilities in delivery of the national curriculum, and it may be that this 'phase team' leader's job description was simply set out badly, even though the language of this particular school's details indicated a strongly managerialist flavour.

The second strand related to curriculum leadership or co-ordination with reference to a particular subject: usually for one of the 'core' subjects of English, maths and science, but occasionally for information technology. This was the most common kind of set of responsibilities for both 'B'/2 and 'A'/1 posts. It was not possible to distinguish between levels of seniority by reference to the subjects for which the post was responsible: English/Language, Maths, Science, Technology, Music and Humanities all appeared as both 'A'/1 and 'B'/2 posts. PE only appeared as an 'A'/1 responsibility. In addition, it was clear that in some schools almost all the subject co-ordination was undertaken by main grade/standard scale teachers.

Only one school stated a clear distinction between the two grades of allowance. All teachers had classroom responsibilities. Main grade teachers would also have a designated responsibility area which 'could be' a subject area, and would be expected to 'show an interest' in developments, working 'with support' to influence practice. 'A' postholders would have a curriculum area responsibility, take a leading role in curriculum discussions, initiating these when appropriate, and be responsible for budget and resource decisions in their area. They would be expected to monitor and evaluate practice in their area. 'B' postholders would do all this, but for two curriculum areas or one curriculum and one management area (these were not defined). In addition, they would be expected to contribute to in-service training and to initiate new developments in this from a whole-school perspective.

Even when posts with similar titles in different schools received the same responsibility allowance, the duties assigned to the posts could be quite different. Thus, two 'B' allowances were given for posts of early years co-ordinator. Both would have responsibilities for revising, updating and reviewing the guidelines and schemes of work, and for arranging in-service training in their areas for colleagues. Apart from those agreed responsibilities, there was significant divergence. One was deemed to be a member of the senior management team. She or he would have responsibility for developing assessment and records of achievement for the early years; for display in the early years classes and school area; and for monitoring the use of resources. None of these responsibilities or statements about seniority in the school was made about the other early years co-ordinator. Instead, this post would have responsibility for curriculum development, which was differentiated in some unstated way from the curriculum responsibilities they shared; for public relations and relations with parents; for pastoral care; and for establishing and reviewing targets for the staff in the early years classes. In addition, this job description stated that the postholder would have responsibilities for good communication within the school. This kind of variation in the expectations being laid upon holders of apparently similar posts was strongly apparent in the details of posts of Co-ordinator of Special Educational Needs received in 1994, all of which carried two extra points, but had little else in common!

3. How the 'A' posts were viewed

Three-fifths of the 'A'/1 posts were seen as middle management, but this was more common among smaller schools: three-quarters of the heads of schools with ten or fewer staff saw them as middle managers, whereas over half of the remaining schools did not. The relevance of the term was sometimes questioned by heads of smaller schools on grounds of size: the headteacher quoted earlier in the chapter was one of these. The range of responsibilities for 'A'/1 posts was frequently greater in these smaller schools than it was for the 'B'/2 postholders in medium to large schools, and included a substantial variety of duties. One school only gave a single point on a rotating basis to teachers who had temporary responsibility for setting up the new schemes of work for whichever subject or subjects of the national curriculum were due to start the following year. All its permanent promoted positions were '+2's. One 'A' post was that of second to the head in a two-teacher school. As we said above, however, the most common 'A' position was that of a subject specialist or curriculum leader in a particular area.

4. What specific tasks were allocated to postholders?

The job specifications examined cited 626 specific tasks through which postholders were expected to carry out their management roles and functions. It was possible to reduce these to 108 different tasks, categorised under seven headings. These categories are listed in order of frequency of citation in Table 5.1.

However, although subject-related and cross-curricular duties were cited more often than any others, the tasks cited vary enormously within each category, with many being cited only once. In fact, of the 108 different duties categorised, only ten were cited in job descriptions twenty times or more. However, these accounted for 54.5 per cent of all citations. Another eight received ten or more mentions. These eighteen tasks accounted for over 70 per

Table 5.1 Categories and frequency of duties and tasks in primary postholders' job-specifications

Category	No. of tasks/ duties	% of all citations
Subject-related	31	45.7
Cross-curricular/whole-school duties	38	22.6
External relations and relations with parents	6	8.6
Team leadership/interpersonal skills	18	8.1
Staff development	3	7.0
Assessment and records of achievement	8	5.2
Teaching duties	4	2.7

cent of all those cited, which suggests that there is more consistency about the tasks allocated to 'A'/1 and 'B'/2 postholders than the variations between individual job descriptions might indicate. Details are given in Table 5.2, where the number of citations in each survey and overall are given as percentages of the total citations made.

While these figures show substantial consistency between the 1991/3 and 1994 data, four duties showed a marked difference in their ranked importance as judged either by the number of times they were cited, or when the frequency of citation was seen as a percentage of all citations. They are shown in Table 5.3.

The changing importance of 'curriculum development' as a task may be important when we note that two other curricular responsibilities, for monitoring, reviewing, evaluating and updating and for preparing and monitoring guidelines, remain almost constant, declining from a total of 10.6 per cent of citations to 10.2 per cent. This suggests that by 1994 responsibility for 'curriculum development' implies too much teacher-autonomy in the light of

Table 5.2 Eighteen tasks/duties most frequently cited in primary postholders' job descriptions

Task/duty	1991/3 %	1994 %	Overall %
INSET	7.7	9.9	8.8
Review, update, monitor use of, and order resources	5.9	11.5	8.6
Monitor, review, evaluate and update curriculum	5.3	6.6	5.9
Liaison with outside agencies, support services, etc.	2.5	9.2	5.8
Advising/assisting others, specialist expertise	5.6	5.0	5.3
Cross-curriculum liaison	5.0	4.3	4.6
Monitoring curriculum and preparation of guidelines	5.3	3.6	4.5
Curriculum development	7.1	1.3	4.3
Senior member of curriculum team/ active in senior management team	4.3	2.6	3.5
Class teacher	4.3	2.0	3.2
Assessment and records of achievement	2.2	4.0	3.0
Co-ordinating subject throughout school	1.5	3.6	2.6
Promoting parental involvement	3.1	1.7	2.4
Conversant with national curriculum	1.2	3.0	2.1
Lead by example in teaching	1.2	2.6	1.9
Reference to existing LEA/school policies	2.2	1.7	1.9
Leading team in delivery and implementation	1.5	2.0	1.8
Planning, delivering, monitoring and recording work	1.9	1.3	1.6

Table 5.3   Duties showing marked difference in ranked importance between 1991/3 and 1994 surveys

	1991–3 %	1994 %	Difference in rank 1994 over 1991–3	Difference 1994 over 1991–3
Liaison with outside agencies, support services, etc.	2.5%	9.2%	+8	+6.7%
Class teacher	4.3%	2.0%	−5	−2.3%
Curriculum development	7.1%	1.3%	−18	−5.8%
Review, monitor use of, and order resources	5.9%	11.5%	+2	+5.6%

the problems of implementing the national curriculum. On the other hand, the change in balance between the more specific curricular duties, with guidelines giving way to a broader duty to monitor, review and update the curriculum, may reflect the anticipation in Spring 1994 that the Dearing report would require schools to review their curriculum schemes and policies in a less directive manner.

Curriculum responsibilities were clearly less important overall in 1994 than earlier, falling to 11.5 per cent of citations from 17.1 per cent. Assisting colleagues to keep up to date, providing support and in-service training remained fairly constant, rising slightly from 13.3 per cent of all citations to 14.9 per cent. Two areas of work replaced the specifically curricular duties in importance: managing and ordering resources, up from 5.9 per cent to 11.5 per cent and the most commonly cited responsibility in 1994, and liaison with a variety of external agencies and organisations, from secondary schools to local authority support services, which rose from 2.5 per cent to 9.2 per cent. Both suggest a possibly significant delegation of responsibility by the head under the impact of local management, although the importance of external liaison may be inflated in the 1994 figures by the increased number of postholders with specific responsibilities for children with Special Educational Needs.

Although we commented earlier that 'B'/2 posts could be categorised for the most part as either whole-school-focused or subject-related, only two of the commonly cited duties in Table 5.2 demonstrate a whole-school, rather than a sectional responsibility. Cross-curriculum liaison scored a steady 4 to 5 per cent of citations, while being a member of a senior curriculum team or senior management team accounted for 3.5 per cent of the total. Interestingly, this figure was lower in 1994 than earlier. In most cases the detailed duties required under cross-curriculum liaison were strongly focused on single-subject responsibilities, involving the postholder in checking other schemes of work to ensure that there were no overlaps or gaps in coverage. 'Co-ordinating a subject throughout the school' is a sectional rather than a genuinely cross-curricular responsibility. However, there is also a cross-curricular duty within the most frequently cited responsibility overall: for INSET. In the overwhelming majority of cases, this involved responsibility for providing in-service in one's subject area, but a small number of 'B'/2 post job descriptions included responsibility for planning in-service training for the school as a whole. This often stated that the in-service wishes of the subject-leaders should be met so far as possible: a proper whole-school responsibility.

The language of most job descriptions spoke of co-ordination and assistance rather than management. It was frequently stated that policy formation, curriculum development and the writing of guidelines should be done in collaboration with other teachers. Further, although there was a strong emphasis on providing advice and assistance to other staff, and on providing or arranging for in-service training, there was little emphasis on providing leadership in the task or trying to ensure conformity, although they became more common in 1994. Further, there were few references to building and sustaining teamwork, except as a member of a senior management team. There was, however, reference to providing support and assistance to colleagues, a responsibility which received over 5 per cent of all citations. Almost no job description spoke of the postholder having responsibility for implementing policies or decisions.

The responsibilities outlined here were found in job descriptions for both 'A'/1 and 'B'/2 postholders in a random sample of primary schools drawn from all over England and Wales and ranging in size from 29 to 600 pupils. They suggest that the curriculum postholder is still the norm, even though the responsibility for aspects of the work of colleagues can now be allocated to teachers without responsibility allowances. Since the survey did not collect job descriptions for any posts not carrying an allowance it was difficult to identify any obvious difference between the kinds of responsibilities being laid down for postholders and those being asked of teachers who were receiving no additional payment for their work outside the classroom. It also appears that whole-school responsibilities are limited, for the most part, to those which surround curriculum co-ordination, although this may be less true now than it was even two years ago, with more teachers receiving two additional responsibility points being seen as senior management. It would also seem that the relationship between postholders and their colleagues is not, for the most part, seen as one which allows the postholder to require any kind of conformity from others, and supports Campbell's (1985) analysis of the curriculum co-ordinator's role.

5. What is expected of postholders?

Most job particulars included either a formal person specification – a statement of the characteristics and experience which the successful candidate will possess – or a less formal statement of what will be expected of applicants. These details were reinforced by the short questionnaire. Once again, there was no strong pattern to be found in what was being looked for, but we can identify one or two important changes.

Questionnaire data suggested that heads advertising in 1994 were looking for teachers who have more ambition than earlier. For '+1' posts upwards of two years experience was wanted, whereas for 'A' allowances it could be up to twelve years. For a '+2' post, with one exception heads expected three to five years in a promoted post compared with anything from three years to 'at least ten' years for 'B's. All heads wanted the person appointed to stay for at least two years and most hoped for three or four. The big difference was what was expected at the end of that time. Whereas most 'A' and '+1' posts were seen as leading to promotion, only one-quarter of 'B' posts were seen in the same way, compared with almost half of the '+2' posts.

Every head wanted to appoint a teacher who had taught across the full range of children in that school, and some infant and junior schools expressed interest in teachers who had taught across the full primary range. Just under half of the respondents who were advertising 'B' positions in 1991–3 wanted previous managerial experience, compared with only 15 per cent of the heads offering '+2's in 1994, and only 10 per cent of 'A'/1 advertisers. Interestingly, in spite of the statement in the teachers' conditions of service schedule that all teachers would have some managerial or co-ordinating responsibility for the work of other teachers, only two schools stated that all their teachers had managerial responsibilities. However, one-quarter of all schools responding in 1991–3 stated either that some standard scale teachers had middle management functions or that standard scale teachers sometimes had to carry these out, whereas only one school stated that this was the case in 1994.

The further particulars sent to applicants were less consistent even than the responses to the questionnaires. 265 different statements were made concerning previous experience (86), the attitude of teachers towards their colleagues and to matters of policy and philosophy (104), qualifications (30) and subject knowledge (45). Considering that the majority of the posts were for curriculum responsibilities, this last figure is, perhaps, surprising. Indeed, only 21 posts referred to it, while another 12, all infant/first school posts, required knowledge of language acquisition in early years. In examining qualifications, 13 demanded qualified teacher status, 10, recent in-service training, and another 7, that the candidate had or was working for further professional qualifications.

The real variation came in considering the experience and attitudes sought. This to some extent might be seen as contradicting the earlier comments from the job specifications on the lack of attention to team development and leadership. The most commonly sought personal qualifications and attitude were found in requests for leadership qualities, a commitment to teamwork and experience of having worked in teams. These were sought for both 'A'/1 and 'B'/2 posts. In addition, twenty advertisers sought organisational or curriculum leadership experience. The only other aspects of professional experience which were fairly widely sought were evidence of high quality classroom practice – by fifteen advertisers – and previous involvement in providing in-service training for colleagues – sought for nine posts. Interestingly, this was sought from teachers applying for 'A'/1 posts as well as for more senior positions, so this suggests that main/standard scale teachers were being expected to provide this kind of support and assistance as well as receiving it from promoted postholders.

6. What makes a primary school post 'middle management'?

It is extremely difficult to identify from these data the characteristics of a 'middle management' post which could be applied to most of the schools which responded to the survey. This was borne out by the responses to the question which asked the headteachers to state the characteristics of a job that made it, in their view, a 'middle management' position. Many simply avoided the question. We have left aside four heads who simply declared that all promoted postholders were middle management by virtue of holding a responsibility allowance. Other than these, 44 different characteristics were reported, of which eighteen were mentioned only once each. Table 5.4 shows those listed three times or more.

This list suggests that for most primary heads, 'middle management' involves a key curriculum responsibility, possibly leading a team of teachers in its planning and delivery, and providing some assistance and in-service training. The only respondent who sought to differentiate clearly between senior and middle management agreed with this view, stating that middle management was concerned with the curriculum, while senior management had responsibilities beyond the curriculum, and belonged to a senior management team, which provided a forum for discussion, leadership of the year groups, and a close involvement in all aspects of the school. This, however, stands completely at odds with those respondents who saw middle management as involving wider

Table 5.4 Heads' statements about the characteristics of middle management posts

Is co-ordinator of a curriculum area, particularly a key/core area	15
Will lead, guide and/or advise a team, and promote discussion	15
Shares management responsibility with the head and deputy and other postholders under the authority of the head, or acts as general assistant to the head and deputy	10
Is a member of a senior planning team/senior management team/policy team/school development planning team	10*
Records progress/oversees continuity and progression and reports to the senior management team; has regular contact with the senior management team	8
Has some staff development responsibilities, including leading INSET and the introduction of new ideas	7
Has whole-school responsibilities and liaises with other postholders	6
Has responsibility for the management and deployment of resources	5
Has additional responsibilities beyond the curriculum	5
Is a link between the head/deputy head and the staff	5
Has a whole-school overview	4
Has cross-curricular responsibilities	3

* This number may be inflated by apparent confusion in some of the responses. It was found that some heads were able to declare a post to be middle management in one part of the questionnaire and then to state that its incumbent was a member of the senior management team two questions further on. Consequently, it was not clear whether this membership of a senior management team or planning team was truly seen as a middle management characteristic.

responsibilities beyond the curriculum. Generally speaking, the relationship with senior staff in the school, and the extent to which wider school responsibilities beyond the narrow curriculum focus are seen as a part of the middle management function, is not clear. Nor do we have a clear picture from this question, or from the other data, about how these teams are constituted or expected to function.

The characteristics mentioned only once or twice further confuse the picture, and also show some of the confusion surrounding the roles of promoted postholders. Individual heads saw the crucial element of a middle management role in their school as involving such diverse considerations as having fewer precise administrative jobs to do than senior management; promoting parents' events; being involved in appraisal; influencing colleagues to adopt new classroom management approaches which would lead to the adoption of teacher assessment of pupil achievement; researching and disseminating new initiatives; needing a broad overview of the place of the subject in the school and possessing the professional skills and personality to help teachers perform better; having to manage personnel (everyone, in this head's school, having curriculum management responsibilities); needing to be consulted about decisions affecting the whole school; and having a stronger element of accountability in their work. For these respondents, middle management appears to vary between basic administration and a wide-ranging involvement in generating new classroom practice.

Activity 5.2

If you have not done this as you have read through this chapter, it would be a good idea before you go on to compare your view of the promoted postholders' duties and responsibilities with the picture presented above. Are there any people in your school who, on the basis of what has been said in this chapter, you would now regard as 'middle management'? If there are, how would you differentiate their work from that of other teachers who are not middle managers?

6

Primary School 'Middle Management' in Action: Some Case Studies

The four case studies which follow attempt to strengthen our picture of the work involved in carrying out 'middle management' roles in primary schools. They are representative of a range of interviews conducted in small to middle-sized primary schools within one shire county, and allow us to investigate what the postholders themselves saw their roles as being, how they carried out the various tasks they had, and how far they saw themselves as carrying out 'management' tasks. They also begin to move us from considering what management requires, how our view of it is constructed, and what influences it to questions of how we might do what is required. They date from the period 1991–3, when primary schools were implementing substantial changes in curriculum and assessment which required postholders to re-appraise their management responsibilities. Their relevance was tested by circulating them among other primary school postholders in 1994/5, who have confirmed that they remain accurate portrayals of 'middle management' in action. All the names, of course, are pseudonyms.

There are no activities in this chapter. However, I suggest that as you read each case study you bear in mind the following questions:

- What similarities can I identify between this person's situation and my own in terms of school setting, responsibilities, and colleagues' expectations/attitudes?
- In what ways does the case differ from my situation?
- How similar is my view of my management responsibilities (or those I hope soon to hold) to that of this case study subject?
- Where there are particular activities or events described in the case study, would I have done them differently in my school? If so, why?

At the end of each case, you should ask yourself:

- What does this case study teach me about my approach to management responsibilities, and about the expectations of my colleagues and senior management? What changes or re-appraisals ought I to consider to my practice?

CASE STUDY 1: SYLVIA EARNSHAW

Sylvia Earnshaw had taught in six schools over some thirty years, the last thirteen of which had been at an eight-class aided infants school of 220 children with four teachers in each of years R/1 and 2. She had held an 'A' allowance for the last four years. Her job description gave her responsibility for 'staff leadership' in the development of design and technology, the production of a school policy document for this area and the selection, allocation and storing of appropriate curricular resources. She also had administrative responsibilities for ordering, storing and allocating art and paper materials, which were a legacy of her previous responsibility for Art, responsibility for liaising with another member of staff in organising school displays, and some external liaison with the residents of a nearby block of flats. She was responsible to the deputy head for arranging playground duty and hall assembly rotas, and to the newly promoted curriculum manager (a 'B' post) for the induction of all new staff.

Sylvia stated that her overriding concern was to help her colleagues rather than to direct them, although she would 'pull rank' if necessary to ensure that the technology policy was carried out. However, she would not do this if the result was likely to be 'uproar': instead, she would discuss what should be done with the head or deputy. Equally, she would expect a senior colleague to consult her on a technology issue before acting.

'Helping' rather than 'directing' her colleagues generated a number of activities and strategies. She had to keep up-to-date on national curriculum requirements and on published and advocated 'best practice' so that she could inform her colleagues on classroom approaches and help them plan their work. She had introduced the teaching of technology through a series of after-school workshops, which had built up her colleagues' confidence in the area, and by exploring existing teaching in the school which had arisen out of a course on visual arts she had undertaken four or five years previously. She felt that once the teachers were confident about what 'technology' was she could create a formal curriculum statement which would reflect national curriculum requirements.

Her approach to developing the policy document, she said, would be to sketch out the 'bare bones' of a policy and promote general discussion of the area in staff meetings, before preparing a document which she would go through with the curriculum manager. This was partly because of her colleague's curriculum leadership role, and partly because they were good friends and could share ideas openly. The document would go back to the staff for further discussion before being finalised. In this way, said Sylvia, the policy document would be 'everybody's document'.

Sylvia was also responsible for materials. Mobile trolleys for science and technology materials had been created, and staff either took the trolley to the classroom or signed materials out. She needed to tighten up on her monitoring of materials use as staff were somewhat casual about signing materials in and out. However, incorrect or over-use soon became apparent when staff complained that materials were not available! This arrangement also encouraged teachers to plan their teaching collaboratively so as to maximise resources availability across each year group. This collaboration was helped by their ability to work together in a close and supportive school. She did not ask colleagues to teach particular aspects of technology each term; instead, she sought its proper integration into the topics being taught, and to ensure coverage of all necessary elements over the two years of infant school. Neither did she see herself as seeking to impose a particular teaching approach, although she did believe that if necessary she could insist on particular work being done or approaches being taken. It seems, therefore, that she saw herself as accountable to the head for the teaching of technology at the school, and therefore saw her colleagues as accountable to her for their teaching of 'her' subject area.

She was able to take the low-key, enabling line for a number of reasons. One was the supportive and collaborative culture of the school, shown for example by the willingness of year one teachers to shoulder extra duties while their year two colleagues dealt with key stage 1 testing. Another was the size of the school, and the fact that there were four teachers working with each year group. There was also a great deal of discussion about what people were doing, and great openness. Colleagues looked at each others' classrooms and knew what others were doing. In addition, she collated copies of the topics which individual teachers were doing, which were open for everyone to see. And her oversight of display work helped her to see what her colleagues were doing.

Her attempts to influence her colleagues' practice were both overt and informal. The formal workshops have already been mentioned. The other approach was simply to 'pop in a suggestion' when talking. Since staff were reasonable and open to suggestion, she could exploit casual conversations for this. Indeed, they were prepared actively to seek assistance or advice from one another. It was also possible to offer to help, as she had done with a colleague whose displays were 'absolutely appalling'.

She acknowledged all five 'scientific management' functions – planning, organising, co-ordinating, commanding and controlling – although the last two were carried out obliquely rather than directly. Thus she planned the school displays, but saw herself as undertaking less direct planning of technology at this stage – it was more of a 'step-by-step' approach, she said. Organisation was obviously a task, especially in relation to the materials for technology teaching. Co-ordination, essential in order to ensure proper skill-progression for the children, was achieved through her organisation of materials and resources. She objected to command – 'such a strong word,' she said – and also to control, but acknowledged that she asked for action, checked that it was done, and brought pressure to bear on colleagues if it was not.

As the teacher responsible for technology and display, Sylvia Earnshaw had to exercise a range of managerial functions. She also acknowledged forms of accountability to colleagues and to the head and a 'B' postholder for her work. What was crucial to understanding her work was less the responsibilities she carried than how she performed them, and this was strongly influenced by the character and size of the school. Cultural influences were critical: she did not have to be directive, but recognised that direction was her responsibility; she could depend on willing collaboration and involvement. Her concern in developing technology teaching was to reassure, to involve, and to establish ownership of the programme by her colleagues, rather than to instruct, to direct and to monitor in a bureaucratic structure.

CASE STUDY 2: WENDY OSBORNE

Wendy Osborne held an 'A' allowance as Lower School Co-ordinator and School Assessment Leader at a small village school of 120 children, with five staff and a non-teaching head who nevertheless taught extensively to provide cover and release for the staff when needed. The school is designed in two 'sides' linked by the assembly hall/gym. The key stage 2 classes are in a traditional classroom side, while the key stage 1 children are taught in an open-plan area. It was her second post, and she was in her second full year at the school when interviewed.

Her job description gave her responsibility for overseeing the implementation of key stage 1, for assessment throughout the school, for pre-school group liaison, and for taking the lead in developing whole-school policies for 'the topic approach' and RE. She was expected to do this by supporting staff through school-based INSET and disseminating information from LEA courses, keeping abreast of developments and assisting staff with record-keeping; organising the administration of SATs and providing necessary support to the teachers involved in them. Her responsibilities for 'topic' and RE also included oversight and staff development in the use of resources.

So far she had focused her energies on implementing key stage 1 and on assessment and records of achievement in the school. She had worked closely on assessment for her first year with another 'A' postholder who had now moved on to promotion, and she had had responsibility for the deployment of staff during the key stage 1 testing period.

The most difficult aspect of her work was the uncertainty which surrounded the development of assessment and records of achievement, with government directives tentative and subject to change. Because of this, she found herself working in close collaboration with the head, who could take time to study materials and directives and provide an additional opinion. The danger that her colleagues might be asked to introduce changes only to have them superseded by revisions to government or county policy meant that any proposals needed more weight than her position alone could give them. However, in general this was not the case: she described the school as open and collaborative, with a strong emphasis on the team and a systematic use of regular staff meetings to develop and establish policies for the school as a whole.

If environmental uncertainty created the most difficult aspect of Wendy's work, the most important, in her view, was co-ordinating practice and disseminating information. She wished to ensure that all the staff working with years R, 1 and 2 were fully in touch with one another and informed about developments. The deputy head also taught key stage 1, and the two of them liaised closely with one another and with the head. The three of them saw working together as a team as an important example of good practice to their colleagues. Keeping each other up-to-date and considering the implications of developments for key stage 1 teaching or assessment, led to extensive discussion of classroom practice and management, which increased knowledge of one another's teaching styles, and further generated a team culture. This was helped by the open-plan nature of their side of the school. Wendy felt there was less of a team culture in the key stage 2 side, partly because she did not teach there, partly because of physical layout, and partly because of the head's policy of keeping assessment procedures constant for a cohort of children throughout their career at the school. Consequently, the changes were only being introduced at key stage 1.

As it was such a small school, every member of staff had curriculum responsibilities, and Wendy had to disseminate information and ensure that colleagues were properly informed and up-to-date, especially concerning assessment. She did not try to filter or direct information; in such a small school, everyone needed to know about developments, since they had to work collaboratively as a team. This also meant that decisions on which innovations or initiatives should have priority had to be taken by the whole staff together, not by individual postholders.

Wendy did not accept that she had any formal responsibility as a postholder for the work of other staff. She said she was not responsible for monitoring how her colleagues were implementing agreed policies on records of achievement and assessment. She did recognise some informal responsibility as team leader for the work of the key stage 1 team, but this was mainly in terms of ensuring that the team was working collaboratively and keeping in step. She would consider taking unsatisfactory work from a colleague to the headteacher, but commented that as the only member of staff not teaching full time, he was more likely to be aware of problems in the classroom and bring them to her attention than vice versa. The only formal accountability which she acknowledged was to the head, who had to agree the planned schemes of work for each term with each teacher, and received and filed copies of the agreed programme. Consequently, implementation of the agreed scheme was a matter between the head and the individual.

Her intended approach to developing an RE policy reflected her concern for teamwork and resistance to taking responsibility for others' teaching. She planned to put a draft paper to a staff meeting, then revise and re-present it in the light of comments. The staff meeting discussion was important, since all the staff except the head were classroom teachers and so did not see each other in action. Both formal staff meetings and informal staffroom conversation demonstrated, however, that the school's teachers were prepared to talk openly about what they did and their successes and problems. Thus staff meetings would provide open and genuine feedback on what was wanted, and agreement at a staff meeting on a particular policy or course of action would, she believed, lead to genuine attempts to implement it.

Wendy recognised both planning and organising dimensions to her role, especially concerning the administration of SATs and making cover arrangements. Co-ordinating colleagues' work was limited to pupil assessment, record-keeping, and working timetabling arrangements for activities such as music. She saw herself as monitoring others' work only to assist in her own planning. It was achieved through discussion, and, occasionally, when the head covered her class to release her to work alongside a colleague. She did not accept that she should evaluate others' work, nor that she could either command or control it. If someone was departing significantly from the agreed key stage 1 programme, it would, she said, be a matter for a whole-staff meeting, and she would bring this about by taking it up with the head if he did not initiate the discussion himself.

Wendy Osborne's approach to her managerial role was strongly influenced by the size of the school, the attitudes she attributed to the head, and her perception of her professional relationships with her colleagues. The school was small, and so directive relationships were inappropriate: collaboration and willing co-operation was seen as the only satisfactory basis on which to build a culture of unity which was essential for such a small group. The head's emphasis on open discussion and team-building strengthened if it did not directly shape her belief that the proper way of working was through consent, and was in line with her view that individuals were essentially autonomous and had to join a group by their own acceptance of its authority to influence what they did. This sense of teacher autonomy led her to believe that even when working collaboratively individuals were responsible for their own work and not directly accountable to her in a hierarchical relationship, and this affected both what she felt able to do and how she felt entitled to act in pursuit of the tasks she had to perform.

CASE STUDY 3: GRAHAM ILIFFE

Graham Iliffe held a 'B' allowance in a 1.5-form-entry aided primary school with just over 300 children on roll. It was oversubscribed and had a strong local reputation. This was his fourth teaching appointment: previously he had worked in two comprehensive schools and then at a junior school. He preferred to work in a primary school because the smaller size created a greater sense of team and community spirit, the children were more responsive, and he could teach a greater variety of subjects.

Graham's job description began by stating that he was to be 'part of the management team', and then that he was to 'lead by example in the classroom' through good management and stimulating displays. He was to promote maths in the school by example in the classroom, advising and working alongside colleagues, running workshops for them and evenings for parents, being part of a team developing and implementing a maths policy, resourcing and monitoring the use of a maths area, ordering materials, building a maths library for staff, advising on maths courses for possible staff development, attending in-service programmes himself, and keeping abreast of national developments. He was also expected to liaise with local secondary schools, maths resource centres, and other agencies. He had to undertake lunchtime supervision, take assemblies as requested, and take full responsibility for ordering, monitoring and dispensing all consumable stock. This last responsibility was closely monitored by the head, who required him to give out stock to staff on a weekly basis, and to keep the stock cupboard locked at all other times. He had also just been given the task of being curriculum leader for PE. However, staff at the school stated that curriculum leadership duties were not the basis of an allowance, and Graham declared that his allowance was held for his management responsibilities and his responsibility for resources.

Even so, he had only become involved in management team meetings and discussions to any significant extent in the preceding two terms, having devoted most of his attention to his mathematics responsibilities in his first two years in post. In his view 'management' was quite distinct from his curriculum responsibilities, involving a whole-school perspective and creating a policy overview, whereas his curriculum duties were more like 'little boxes that can be taken separately and worked on'. However, it clearly included some of the administrative duties which had a whole-school focus, and his freedom of action here appeared quite significantly constrained by the close oversight of his actions exercised by the headteacher.

Perhaps because he had relatively recently been fully incorporated into the management team, Graham had difficulty in explaining in detail what its work involved. An important task for the management team was deciding on the priority areas for curriculum development work. Thus in the term that he was interviewed, much work had been done on the maths curriculum, and history and geography were scheduled for the following term. However, as his subsequent account of his work on the maths curriculum showed, most of the work appeared to be done by the curriculum postholder, and the management team's involvement was hard to identify.

Although his responsibility for the maths curriculum was not, in his view, enough on its own to merit an allowance, Graham indicated that it had absorbed a great deal of time. He had judged it necessary when he came to create a completely new maths policy, and scheme of work, a statement which appeared to contradict his earlier claim that the management team determined the curriculum development priorities. He said that it was only now that this major review and innovation had been completed that he had been taken fully into the management team's deliberations.

He approached the process of policy revision by drafting a document which was then discussed in detail at a sequence of staff meetings. Changes were incorporated into the document which was then accepted and established as policy. Graham stated that there were some staff who would prefer to have the subject co-ordinator impose a policy for them to follow, but said that he felt that was wrong, and that consultation was important. Consequently, he omitted elements of the policy to ensure that discussion would develop, so that he could find out everybody's opinions from the debate.

He adopted a similar approach when considering the new scheme of work for maths, devoting a full half term to getting teachers to look at their own maths schemes and examine alternatives before coming to a decision to order different schemes for each key stage. He did this because the key stage 2 staff were very keen on a scheme which the key stage 1 teachers disliked intensely, and Graham felt that there was good enough progression from one to the other to make the compromise workable. One key stage 2 teacher who was not too keen on the scheme finally chosen said that she was quite happy to go along with whatever was decided, so long as it *was* decided.

Graham's approach to consultation was quite different with the two groups of staff. The key stage 2 teachers got on well together, and also included all the holders of permanent allowances, whereas the four key stage 1 staff included two strong personalities who did not get on well together. Consequently, he was happy to discuss the question in open meetings of the key stage 2 staff, where people would express their opinions but were ready to compromise. With the key stage 1 teachers, he worked through individual discussions until there was some apparent agreement, before bringing them together to examine a possible scheme – which was chosen.

As the subject co-ordinator, Graham was responsible for monitoring maths teaching in the school. This was a sensitive task, since although some of the staff were able to agree on actions and policies they were reluctant to accept someone coming into the classroom to see what they were doing. He put this down to perfectionism: uncertain if their work reached their own ideal standards, he saw them as fearful of their self-criticism being confirmed by a third party. Consequently, he felt unable to monitor as much as he would wish, nor to see decisions through into action. Monitoring was done indirectly, looking over exercise books and admiring displays, and noting what he saw on the blackboard. However, he was not responsible for ensuring the progress of individual children, nor were his colleagues accountable to him for their maths teaching. He did not feel that he should be involved in the liaison and co-ordination arrangements which existed between teachers who were teaching the same age children, and which resulted from the mixed-age classes made necessary by the school's 1.5 forms of entry. Indeed, his view of his curriculum role was as a facilitator. He listed five elements of the post: responsibility for resources, responsibility for staff development in maths, liaison with external agencies, going on maths courses himself and disseminating information, and assisting colleagues if they had difficulties in teaching maths. This perception of his primary task as a subject co-ordinator matched that of the job description, which spoke of his duties as being part of a team – but not, formally at least, a leader of it – responsible for developing maths policies and schemes, and providing to colleagues an example of outstanding practice to emulate.

The distinction drawn between monitoring and evaluating the maths teaching in the school showed clearly Graham's perceptions of the limits of authority of a postholder. He saw teachers as autonomous professionals, accountable to colleagues other than the head only in so far as they had conceded elements of their autonomy freely and by their own consent. The policy document was quite detailed and laid down a range of activities to be covered in each year of the children's career, which is why he wanted it agreed rather than imposed. However, failures to deliver the approved policy, refusals to teach what was agreed, or cases of unsatisfactory teaching would be referred to the headteacher to deal with. Even as a member of the management team, Graham did not feel that he possessed the authority to act.

Graham acknowledged responsibility for planning, organising and co-ordinating but struggled with the idea that he might have to command or control. He planned the new maths policy and scheme, and organised all the teaching resources. He had to co-ordinate their use, and also the introduction of the new scheme when it arrived. When asked if he exercised a command function, he said he tried to avoid giving orders, but had the final responsibility in the light of discussions and consultation to decide on which maths scheme to introduce, and, when pressed, that he would have to ensure that the new scheme was followed when it arrived. However, he was clearly uneasy, falling back on a faith in discussion rather than direction, and commenting that he could dictate as part of management, but would probably make any dictation come from the head!

Similarly, he preferred monitoring to control. He said that he could describe how every one of his colleagues taught maths, how they organised their classroom, and the extent to which they expanded their teaching beyond adherence to the textbook, but could not require changes in that practice. He could make suggestions and recommendations on the basis of professional knowledge, but only the head, and perhaps the deputy, could require conformity or change.

Despite his being the most senior of the four cases presented here, Graham's views of the primary postholder's role offered the clearest statement of the tension between planning and implementation duties which came through all the interviews. Primary teachers seemed happy to work on developing plans or policy documents, and felt almost unanimously that colleagues should participate in the development process. But although the need to monitor implementation was recognised, they shied away from it, only undertaking it informally if they undertook it at all. The only person who was seen as having the authority to monitor formally the work of teachers in a school was the headteacher, or, very occasionally, the head and deputy. Even 'B'/+2 postholders who were members of a whole-school or senior management team did not acknowledge this responsibility. Thus in a crucial way the value-system of the primary postholders denied a managerial function, and reinforced the proprietorial view of primary schools demonstrated by Alexander (1984).

CASE STUDY 4: LAURA ARMITAGE

Laura Armitage denied any management role at all. She was an 'A' postholder at a one-form-entry aided primary school of just under 200 children, where she had taught for twenty years. She had held a promoted post there for seven years, and had briefly served as acting deputy head, but personal circumstances had prevented her from applying for the permanent post. She did not provide a formal job description, but stated that she held her allowance for music, and for information technology, computing and maths. The maths work was a recent addition due to staff illness, and she suspected that the computing work was gradually being given to someone else – a suspicion that proved correct.

Her approach to her responsibilities for computers and maths reflected a consistent attitude that her colleagues were highly experienced and overworked professionals who were facing a range of unreasonable demands and should, so far as possible, be left to get on with the job of teaching as they saw best. She believed that her colleagues shared her view that each class was more of a family than a class, and that teachers would no more allow someone to interfere with their teaching than they would let someone tell them how to bring up their family. She remarked that although teachers might listen to ideas about teaching in a staff meeting, they would often be thinking, 'that's fine, but it's not the way I do it.' This view of the classroom as a personal, private kingdom, which she presented very forcefully, matches Lieberman and Miller's (1984) research on primary school cultures.

This view affected her approach to influencing her colleagues' practice, because in spite of her stress on professional autonomy she did ensure that she knew what the other teachers did and sought to influence it. She did this, however, not because she was the teacher in charge of maths, but because she had been for some years the teacher of the year six class. Consequently, she had developed a clear perception of what the children needed to know and be able to do when they arrived in her class, and she wished to ensure that the children were prepared for her.

When she found out that things were being taught that she would need to 'unteach' later, she would approach the question indirectly by 'a passing word', which would avoid direct criticism of the teacher however justified such criticism might be. Rather, she would direct criticism towards the text or materials, in order to suggest alternatives, or that the topic be left and tackled some other time.

Her approach to monitoring what was being taught was necessarily informal, because although the head expected postholders to see their colleagues in action, Laura's responsibilities for teaching music made this difficult. She would monitor by observing what was on display and by 'wandering around' and seeing what the children showed her. She would not go and start leafing through a maths book and commenting on what she found there.

When she had to prepare a maths policy for the school after taking over responsibility for the subject, she wrote a policy which reflected the existing practice and the scheme currently in use. In accordance with the head's decision-making policy on such curriculum documents, it was subjected to detailed scrutiny as part of a staff residential weekend, and there was some amendment at that stage, although she decided beforehand that as she had to take responsibility for the policy she would refuse to compromise on some elements of the document, wherever the pressure for amendment might come from. She was reluctant to make too many formal changes to take account of national curriculum requirements, saying that she preferred to let things settle down before undertaking a major rewrite. However, in accordance with the wishes of the head and deputy, the maths policy and scheme was reviewed formally at a staff meeting at least every term, and Laura kept a careful ear open for any other comment. Consequently, the programme was subject to constant amendment in the light of formal and informal feedback.

Since the school was only small, with seven staff including the headteacher, there was a lot of informal contact, and Laura believed that her informal conversations and passing remarks in the corridor were more revealing and valuable than formal staff meeting discussions, where everyone was extremely careful what they said for fear of what others might think. In particular, just sitting and listening, rather than trying to orchestrate or chair a formal discussion, was often far more informative, because much is said in staffroom conversations that is never written down, and, as she put it, 'when people are just talking they're not always thinking.'

This statement suggests that, for all the small size of the staff and the togetherness and informal contact she described, there was a great deal of distrust and micropolitical tension within the school. It was difficult to determine how far this was her personal perception as a self-confessed 'non-conformist who is tolerated because she gets things done' or a more widespread feeling, and more will be said about this below.

Clearly, then, Laura saw her key function as maths co-ordinator as supporting her colleagues rather than as monitoring and evaluating their work, although she accepted that she did evaluate. This was less important in relation to maths, in which all the staff were competent, than in relation to computing. Here, her perception of staff as essentially autonomous but overburdened professionals was crucial to how she acted.

She had started promoting the use of computers in the classroom quite early, and had been hampered by unreliable hardware and inadequate software. All her colleagues except for the male head and unmarried female deputy were married women with family responsibilities, which she said reduced their opportunities to learn new skills or undertake additional training. Consequently, she had to persuade people to try new and challenging ideas, provide support when things went wrong (which was often!) and offer constant and comprehensive guidance and assistance as well as searching continuously for better software. Although this was clearly frustrating, she said that she did not feel able to pressure her colleagues too hard because she recognised how they were also balancing many commitments, and this reluctance to put too much innovation on to her colleagues has continued.

Indeed, whereas the other postholders profiled here described their work as disseminating or filtering the information coming in from outside, a key dimension of Laura's view of her responsibility was that she should 'soak up' unreasonable pressure from above or outside, and 'mop up' the complaints and woes of her colleagues in relation to her areas of responsibility. She felt that the head was often placing unreasonable demands on the staff by the way that he wished to respond to the flow of changes being imposed by the government at that time, particularly the national curriculum and testing. She believed he wanted to be in the vanguard of the changes locally, whereas she felt that a more sensible response would be to hasten slowly. As teacher governor she had concluded that the head was nervous of being put under pressure by certain governors and so wanted to be seen to be in the vanguard of local schools in implementing government policy.

Laura's picture of her school as both close and intensely micropolitical was confirmed by others, although of course actions were interpreted differently. For example, Laura declared that she kept out of the way of the deputy head because, having been unable even to apply for the post while acting in that capacity, she felt she should not appear to be interfering in the new deputy's job. The deputy saw Laura as acting with bad grace and needing to be left alone, because she obviously resented not being appointed. The deputy saw the school as collegially run, with the head engaging in wide consultation both formally through staff meetings and informally through conversations in staffroom or corridors. Laura saw the meetings as full of coded remarks and the individual, informal conversations as a tactic of 'divide and rule'. Laura claimed that a good deal of informal consultation and advice-seeking occurred, born of a sense that the head could make life difficult for a teacher so they needed to be prepared. She suggested strongly that her long service at the school had given her a power position in the school which created a counter-culture and which was recognised by some of the staff and many parents. All this shows how an individual postholder can act to frustrate, or at least to reduce the effectiveness, of others' policy decisions. Collegiality and politics are often not very far apart.

In this atmosphere of micropolitics, close friendships and informal contact, it was not surprising that Laura denied any management role. Indeed, she said that management was not appropriate to a small, close-knit primary school, for it simply gave grandiose names to common-sense and everyday events and actions. Nevertheless, she acknowledged that she did plan and organise, having set up and established the maths scheme they used and provided resources for the computers. She also acknowledged that the scheme had created a greater sense of co-ordination of the maths teaching among the staff than had been the case hitherto, and that the staff did agree on the pacing and sequencing of maths work across the school, although she was at pains to stress how these agreements were arrived at informally. She strongly denied that she had any command function, and declared that the nearest she came to seeking to control the work of a colleague was occasionally 'leaning quietly on someone'.

The main difference between Laura and the other postholders profiled here is that, whereas the others saw themselves as accountable to the head, Laura appeared to see herself as accountable primarily to the needs and interests of the staff. Whereas the others saw themselves as enabling the other staff to do a good job and work together, Laura appeared to see her prime responsibility as protecting other teachers from unreasonable demands and interference. Her case is interesting, raising questions about the ways in which individual teachers holding positions of responsibility in primary schools resolve a perceived tension between what they believe to be their obligations to their professional colleagues and their contractual responsibilities and accountability laid down in job descriptions.

CONCLUDING COMMENTS ON THE PRIMARY CASE STUDIES

There were both clear consistencies and strong differences between the four case studies reported here. Certain management tasks were universally acknowledged. Postholders had to engage in planning, organising and co-ordinating the work of their colleagues. However, whereas planning was seen as needing to involve colleagues in taking decisions, organising and co-ordinating responsibilities were essentially administrative. Co-ordinating included a responsibility for monitoring others' work, but this was difficult to do except at arms' length because of the lack of non-contact time. It was also disliked.

The dislike of monitoring duties was reflected in the dislike of command and control tasks, which in most cases were rejected: only one of the four reported here was prepared to accept them, and even she acknowledged them obliquely rather than directly. This was, if anything, a higher proportion of acceptance than was to be found in the total set of cases from which these were selected. For most, control and command, if acknowledged at all, were accepted only from the headteacher.

Fundamental to this was a constant tension between public or hierarchical and professional concepts of accountability. Postholders' professional accountability to their colleagues did not allow them to require or direct others to act in particular ways: they could only advise. Others' professional accountability to postholders placed on them an obligation to teach to high standards, but not to follow any set guidelines or schemes of work laid down by the postholder. On the other hand, a headteacher could direct assistant teachers to act in particular ways. There was a hierarchical relationship between heads and assistants, but the hierarchical elements of that authority could not, apparently, be delegated to anyone else. Public accountability was a direct relationship between the individual teacher and the head which did not involve the postholder. Consequently, control and command tasks could not be accepted because they implied that colleagues were accountable to postholders for their teaching, and that the postholders were themselves accountable to the head for what their colleagues did.

In part, this derives from the way primary school teaching is organised. Few primary teachers have much non-contact time to spend with colleagues or in monitoring others' work, whereas most headteachers are still non-teaching heads, covering classes occasionally. Consequently, individual postholders have little opportunity to exercise direct or close control over others' work: only the headteacher can do this. In addition, the complex web of responsibility relationships which is created by working as generalists rather than as subject specialists makes hierarchical authority hard to exercise in the school. The organisation of primary schools encourages a frame of mind in which the individual subject co-ordinators or postholders exercise essentially enabling and guiding functions as agents of the headteacher, but without the authority to require or direct. This creates an unresolved tension for postholders: are they leaders of teams or promulgators of visions?

The organisation of work makes the knowledge and normative power resources at postholders' disposal rest for their exercise on limited consent and acquiescence, and their colleagues possess sufficient power resources of their own to make it difficult for individuals to exercise their own too overtly. Actions seen by colleagues as over-zealous monitoring and control could trigger a response by others within their area of responsibility at the postholder's expense in the classroom. Consequently, there would appear to be a certain minimalism in the exercise of the formal responsibilities of the job descriptions in order to retain professional autonomy.

However, there was strong recognition of a supportive and advisory role, which was one of the most liked aspects of their work. It appeared to give them status among their colleagues which derived from knowledge and normative power resources rather than economic resources or physical coercion. Knowledge rather than office appeared to be the preferred basis of influencing others.

Although great emphasis was placed on working as a team of colleagues, especially in the smaller schools, job descriptions talked of being part of a team rather than providing leadership. The case studies showed how postholders would promote discussion of policy statements and generate debate over the schemes of work, but saw 'leadership' more as facilitating participation in decisions rather than encouraging staff to move in a particular direction. Although Wendy Osborne spoke of a close, team-based relationship with her head and deputy, and Graham Iliffe of his membership of the management team, neither felt that they were therefore putting into practice the head's vision for the school, even though Wendy clearly shared that vision, as did Sylvia Earnshaw. They all claimed that they were facilitators of colleagues in collegial settings, rather than agents of senior management. On the other hand, Laura Armitage saw herself not as bringing together and promoting new developments approved by the head but as buffering her colleagues from what she regarded as unacceptable interference. Her obligation, it appeared, was to her professional association rather than to the headteacher who had formally defined her responsibilities.

How collegial the discussions actually were was difficult to ascertain.

Certainly the rhetoric was always one of collegiality: decisions being taken by whole-staff meetings, proposals being taken away and re-worked before being brought back to full staff meetings for approval, working parties and groups to carry out development work. Careful examination of the case studies, however, suggests that even in the smallest schools this was less than the whole truth. Wendy Osborne, in her school of five staff, handled the key stage 1 staff quite differently from the more traditionally minded key stage 2 teachers. Key stage 1 were engaged in activities which would build a team emphasis and focus, whereas key stage 2 were dealt with individually if at all. Graham Iliffe dealt similarly with the two groups of teachers over the new maths programme, although in his case it was the key stage 1 staff who had to be talked to individually and the key stage 2 who could argue round a table and come to an agreement. Even in these apparently successfully collegiate schools, forms of micropolitical activity reminiscent of the vignettes in Hoyle (1986) were being engaged in to bring about the decisions that were sought.

In Laura Armitage's school, the rhetoric was apparently even further from the reality. Her case presented a clear demonstration of intense levels of distrust between individuals, which may have centred on herself because of her perceived attitude towards the head and deputy, but also indicated how easily attempts at participative and consultative approaches by senior management can hit obstacles which can make the apparent collegiality a sham.

The organisation of work and the culture of autonomous teachers who must consent collectively to change which, in part, results from that organisation, make it difficult to establish hierarchical structures and bureaucratic approaches to management in primary schools, in which a clear 'middle management' role can be defined and carried out. Although middle management responsibilities and functions are being discharged, they are usually diffused through the school and not concentrated in an identifiable stratum or group of teachers. At the same time, the apparent collegiality which is proposed as an alternative to bureaucracies and hierarchies may founder on demands for professional autonomy and micropolitical manoeuvring. Little use has been made of ambiguity theory in these final comments, but it may be that political and ambiguity theories have more to offer primary school postholders as they struggle to understand what their role is and how it may be performed, than the collegiality which is currently advocated so widely.

The nature of 'middle management' in primary schools, then, is critically dependent on the culture of the school, and the concept of teaching held within it. It was clear that the primary teachers interviewed saw one another as professionals, and therefore needing administrative support and advice on practice rather than management, while being accountable only to the agent of outside accountability – the head. This stands at odds with some of the expectations laid upon the head to deliver the national curriculum and achieve high scores at key stages 1 and 2. Individual postholders embarking on middle management training must decide how far they wish to preserve and work within this status quo and how far it is necessary, desirable and feasible to change it. Preserving the status quo leads one towards an emphasis on working as a facilitator and administrator, taking a lead rather than giving it, and placing a strong emphasis on keeping the team together rather than setting it goals. It will stress skills of resource management and what Mintzberg (1990) calls the interpersonal roles of management. An emphasis on leadership skills and the development of skills to discharge managerial functions of command and control will only be of use if the recipient is working in a bureaucratic or political environment or has the means of changing it in that direction.

7

Middle Management and the Secondary School

CAN SECONDARY SCHOOLS HAVE MIDDLE MANAGERS?

Chapter 6 concluded that for a number of reasons the concept of middle management was problematic when applied to primary schools. Many secondary school teachers, including those who hold what are often called 'middle management' posts, also deny the validity of the concept. However, five characteristics of secondary schools generate a need for middle managers, and with it the possibility that they can work divisively against the senior staff as easily as they can work to create a cohesive organisation. These characteristics are school size, the nature of the work, how it is organised, funding, and how teachers themselves think of their work.

Activity 7.1
Before you read on, you should reconsider your stance on whether 'middle management' is an appropriate idea for secondary schools. You might find it useful to make a few notes using the five characteristics just mentioned as headings. Then compare your response to the question with my discussion which follows.

First, then, the *size* of the school. The smallest secondary school is bigger than all but the very largest primary schools: of the hundred secondary schools which replied to the survey undertaken for this book, the smallest had 20 full-time teaching staff, and only six had fewer than 30. The average teaching staff size was 52.6. In addition, there are more paid technicians and other support staff in secondary schools than are to be found in primary schools. Consequently, more people's work has to be organised, and more information about their needs and requirements must be collected and passed to the relevant people responsible for that organisation to take into account. Some arrangement has to be made for that information to be used when organising the work of the staff.

The second consideration is *the nature of the work*. All organisations have to monitor the work of people in them, and provide support and assistance when needed. Unless it is mechanical work which can be checked by looking at outputs, or by some mechanical or electronic means, then larger organisations will create sub-units to achieve this. However, in much of industry and commerce such work is classed 'supervisory' and is not the direct responsibility of 'middle managers'.

Closely related to this is *how the work is organised.* Traditional academic and technical subject boundaries have been strongly resistant to change in secondary schools, and have been reinforced by government policy on the national curriculum since its announcement in 1987. My research (Bennett 1991) found that the department was the key section of the school to which secondary teachers felt an allegiance – what Becher and Kogan (1980) refer to as the 'basic unit' from which their expectations and norms of proper behaviour are drawn. Ball and Bowe (1992) have also suggested that the department has become more important as the national curriculum has been implemented, at the expense of cross-curricular themes in the original plan.

Alongside the academic divisions into subject areas, secondary schools have usually organised a pastoral system to take on board the problems of children in large organisations. Traditionally a combination of guidance and disciplinary functions, there has been a move in the 1980s and 1990s to strengthen the guidance function and develop a teaching focus through programmes of personal and social education, while giving the disciplinary function to the subject departments as a teaching issue. Thus fragmentation is a strong tendency within secondary schools, with all the problems of subject status (Goodson 1983) and tribalism (Becher 1989) which can create and intensify micropolitical divisions within bureaucratic structures.

This organisational arrangement creates a major difference between primary and secondary schools. Primary teachers have to relate to all the teachers who have management or co-ordinating functions for any subject they teach. This creates the complex web of formal relationships referred to earlier: two teachers are quite likely to be both superordinate and subordinate to one another, depending on the area of the curriculum they are concerned with at the time. Thus small, isolated teams are less likely to exist and the possibility of more collegial working increases. Teachers in secondary schools have fewer potential formal relationships than their primary colleagues, because they will work in a pastoral team and one or perhaps two subject teams. The likelihood that such a web of interconnecting relationships will exist is therefore smaller: instead we have a situation ripe for the creation of both formal and informal hierarchies.

This situation is compounded by the *national funding structure for schools* and the consequences this has for teachers' pay and their teaching resources. Schools are funded through formulae based largely on the number of pupils of particular ages on roll. Subject departments are increasingly funded, at least to a basic level, on a similar kind of formula, taking account of the number of pupils of each age studying it, and weighted by some kind of statement of its basic resourcing needs. It is therefore important for departments to compete with each other to gain as many students as possible, up to a maximum for the teachers available. Teachers' salaries, status and promotion prospects are also affected by the size of the school, since although the old regulations linking the number of promoted posts at each level to school size have been abolished, it is for the most part only larger schools which can create the economies of scale needed to release additional money to fund extra salary points. Consequently, in smaller secondary schools, as with many primary schools, some teachers are receiving no financial reward for holding responsibilities which would carry additional payment in larger schools. It therefore becomes important to ensure that 'your' department is large and influential enough to make it unjustifiable for anyone exercising responsibility for the subject not to be paid a suitable allowance.

It will be clear that these factors generate both a need for people to be responsible for the sub-units of the school, and the danger that instead of their operating as parts of a collaborative and cohesive whole, these sub-units may be operating in a fragmented or divisive way. This relates to the questions of culture discussed in Chapter 4, with particular reference to the work of Wise *et al.* (1984), Sackmann (1992) and Bennett (1991).

You will recall that it was suggested that teachers' self-perceptions can be broadly separated into specialists or experts. Specialists are concerned with passing on a set body of knowledge and tend therefore to acknowledge the authority of dictionary knowledge. They might also acknowledge pedagogical direction, such as when to use particular experiments in science – directory knowledge – but are unlikely to acknowledge direction over issues of class control and discipline except in so far as the demands of dictionary knowledge incline them towards particular broad pedagogical strategies. The subject-leader in a department of specialists could expect conformity to the programme, with its particular combination of dictionary and directory knowledge – what is to be taught and how – which is laid down. This can create strongly integrated departmental cultures.

However, departments of specialists need not necessarily be strongly hierarchical. They could consist of a number of different specialists, collaborating in common core teaching in the lower school, such as would be found in many science courses. Thus if the Head of Science, carrying four responsibility points, was a physicist who had to teach some chemistry, it would be accepted that she should defer to the teacher in charge of chemistry on matters of content and approach, even though the chemist was only being paid two extra points. What is important is the values underpinning how decisions get taken about work: the right of one teacher to direct another is acknowledged, on the basis of a combination of subject knowledge and formal responsibility within the system for its teaching.

This value-system creates a set of expectations of the role of the head of department, or any other middle-management or supervisory post, which is quite different from that found in a department of expert teachers, for experts would not accept that another teacher could direct them in what they taught. Experts might seek advice on the basis of acknowledged expertise, but would reject direction, and advice would therefore be sought informally between equals rather than as a subordinate seeking 'help' from a superordinate.

Neither dictionary nor directory knowledge can be assumed among a department of experts, and its existence, when found, is always tentative. The integrationist drive is rarely to be found in expert departments. Consequently, the middle manager responsible for a sub-unit of experts is unlikely to have the coherent and cohesive set of underlying values upon which to draw in carrying out the management task: the departmental culture will be one of differentiation.

This is especially likely to be the case within the pastoral sphere. Because the proper approach to guidance and the teaching of personal and social education is so much a matter of contention, pastoral teams are likely to be less cohesive than most subject departments. Consequently, pastoral unit leaders have to create a coherent and agreed basis for action within large and disparate groups which lack dictionary or directory knowledge, and it may be that much of this work will rest on forms of recipe knowledge, which lacks any clear consensus on values but gives people rules and procedures to follow which may be successful in resolving immediate problems. Bell (1989, 1992), has emphasised the need to negotiate the basic agreements on what is expected of people in the team, and in this work the generation of what Sackmann (1992) called axiomatic knowledge, which integrates dictionary and directory knowledge by creating a common set of values upon which to found agreement on both what is taught and how, is a key leadership task.

We can argue, then, that middle management – some kind of tier of authority which tries to co-ordinate the day-to-day work of the teachers in the various sub-units and integrate them into the overall totality of the school – is a necessary part of secondary school structures. The consequence of the factors outlined here is that secondary schools are more likely to be places of dispute and argument than places of consensus, and individuals are needed who can undertake the responsibility of trying to weld together the often disparate and disputing sub-units into a coherent whole. This function makes it important that senior management should recognise the integrative function of the middle management role and provide opportunities for it to be exercised. In particular, a two-way management of information is important, and as we shall see in the rest of this chapter, there is little reason to believe that senior staff adequately recognise this function.

WHO ARE THE MIDDLE MANAGERS IN SECONDARY SCHOOLS?

Extra allowances above the main scale have existed in England and Wales since the 1950s. For a long time, they were awarded mainly for subject leadership or long service, and leadership often amounted to teaching the bulk of examination classes and advanced work (Edwards 1985). Such teachers were not 'middle managers': Marland (1981) could describe the head of department as 'a senior member of the overall leadership and planning of the school', while Edwards (1985) wrote that the senior history master was numbered among the elders. He was consulted – in so far as consultation was needed in a relatively stable situation – and had a clear stake in the central purposes of the school.

(Edwards 1985, p. A2)

The idea of 'middle management', then, has developed since the mid-1980s, but remains ill-defined. Dobson (1993) found a 'general consensus' among heads and deputies that the division between middle and senior management existed between grades 'D' and 'E'. But at the other end of the scale, what status was accorded to holders of 'A's and 'B's, who were often teachers in charge of subjects?

In the most important research in the field, Earley and Fletcher-Campbell (1989) use middle management interchangeably with head of department or faculty, and do not usually differentiate between heads of large faculties and small departments, although they are rarely concerned with teachers who are in charge of a subject as its only full-time teacher. Bullock's (1988) empirical study equates heads of department and middle management, as does Donnelly (1990). Kemp and Nathan (1989) start by declaring that 'middle management' covers everyone holding an incentive allowance, but then cast the book entirely in terms of the work of a head of a large department, faculty, house or year. However, it may be argued that the managerial task of the teacher with a single responsibility point, who has to undertake almost all the teaching of the subject alone, and then manage the contribution of two or three other teachers, all giving very small amounts of their time to this subject, is every bit as difficult as running a large departmental team, since the major personal commitment of the other teachers is likely to be elsewhere, with their main teaching responsibilities.

There is, then, no clear answer to be obtained from the literature to the question of who constitute secondary school 'middle management'. The implication of the term is that there is a tier of management below them – junior management or supervisory management, perhaps – which would suggest that middle management only operates where there is some kind of integrative structure through which the smaller units communicate with senior management. Thus heads of faculty, and heads of, say, lower and middle school, would form 'middle management' while heads of individual subjects and years would be 'junior management'. Such a distinction can potentially recognise the integrative function of middle management referred to at the end of the previous section, but needs empirical support from job descriptions and case studies.

Evidence that this might be developing, however, is to be found in the third report of the Interim Advisory Committee on Teachers Pay and Conditions (1990). This showed the following distribution of allowances among the 61 per cent of teachers holding them:

Allowance 'A'　　10%
Allowance 'B'　　26%
Allowance 'C'　　6%
Allowance 'D'　　15%
Allowance 'E'　　4%

(*Source:* Campbell and Neill 1991, app. IV)

This suggests that two levels of promoted posts may be emerging: the 'A'/1 and 'B'/2 posts as first-line promotions to responsibilities of a fairly limited nature, working under 'D'/4 postholders as their line managers. Campbell and Neill (1991) distinguished between the hours teachers spent on teaching-related activities and those on what they loosely called 'administration'. They found that teachers on 'B' allowances and below divided their time similarly, while 'D' and 'E' postholders spent similarly less time teaching and more on 'administration', as Table 7.1, extracted from Table 4.12 of their report, shows:

Table 7.1:　Hours spent on teaching and administration by secondary school teachers

Activity	SNS.	A	B	Salary status C	D	E	DH
Teaching	18.4	18.3	17.9	18.2	16.3	15.0	8.8
Administration	15.1	14.7	15.8	19.0	18.7	18.3	31.4
Total time	52.3	53.2	52.2	57.6	55.1	54.8	58.0

Source: Campbell and Neill 1991, p.25.

Much of what they classified as 'administration' was in fact non-teaching but pupil-related activity or time away from professional responsibilities, such as dealing with discipline problems, attending assemblies, break time, or non-contact time not spent working, rather than management or administration as we discussed in Chapter 3. None the less, the combination of the difference between the 'B' and the 'D' workload distribution and the distribution of scale posts suggests that there may be two levels of promoted post developing.

The small number of 'C' allowances appear to take the worst features of both the 'B' and 'D' workloads: their teaching load appears to be higher than that of their 'B' colleagues and their administration load higher than that of 'D' or 'E' allowance holders. Campbell and Neill do not explore this at all, but it needs some further examination to find out who these 'C' postholders are and why their roles should apparently amalgamate the features of those promoted posts on either side of them in seniority.

Activity 7.2

Two activities would be interesting to carry out at this stage. The first is to establish the distribution of allowances and responsibility payments in your school and compare it with the figures given above. The second is to carry out a diary exercise in which you make a note of all your activities over a period of time and establish what percentage of your time is spent on teaching, preparation, other pupil-related matters, and management concerns. These exercises are often done over an extended period of time – usually a week or even two – but even a day would give you some idea of what the balance looks like. This would also give you something against which to compare the survey data which follow. (There is a detailed diary exercise, and a job analysis activity, which you could use for this purpose, in Bennett (1992), pp. 4–7 and 13–14.)

MIDDLE MANAGERS IN SECONDARY SCHOOLS: SOME SURVEY DATA

At the same time as we surveyed primary schools for the data reported in Chapter 5, we carried out two similar surveys of secondary school posts advertised. Unfortunately, secondary heads were more reluctant to respond, some taking the time to compose and sign letters saying how sorry they were to be too busy to respond but not bothering to send back the further particulars asked for. Because the response was so poor, we must be careful not to read too much into the results, which rest on an analysis of responses from 100 schools, but the findings help to develop the discussion of who are middle managers, and give us some detail about the expectations and formal requirements of promoted posts, and the thinking of the senior staff behind them.

WHO ARE SEEN AS MIDDLE MANAGERS?

The heads were asked, first, to indicate whether they regarded the vacant post or posts advertised as 'middle management'. With only one exception, they supported Dobson's (1993) contention that 'E' allowances were senior management positions, and all 'D' and 'C' posts were categorised as middle management. Thereafter the picture becomes cloudy. Approximately three-quarters of all 'B'/2 posts and one-third of 'A'/1 posts were described as middle management, while the rest were not. Most teachers in charge of departments or subject areas were middle managers, but so were the majority of teachers who had defined responsibilities within large departments. Nor did the existence of a faculty structure influence the definition of the status of 'B'/2 posts, even though the lengthened hierarchy might have been expected to have an effect: heads of department on 'B'/2 posts within faculties were still middle managers more often than not. It might be expected, too, that 'B'/2 posts would be less likely to gain middle management status in larger schools, but this was not so: two-thirds of the heads of schools with more than 75 full-time staff stated that teachers holding 'B' allowances or two responsibility points were part of their school middle management.

Heads were asked to indicate who they saw as middle management in their school. Some answers simply spoke in terms of the allowances carried by the middle management posts, with the most common answer, just, being that posts carrying two to four points or their predecessor allowances counted as middle management. A small number of answers identified a clear stratum of section heads, such as heads of department/faculty and heads of year/lower or upper school. It was rare for both heads of year and heads of 'schools' to be bracketed together as middle management, but this frequently happened for faculty and departmental heads. A third category of response gave middle management status to teachers with cross-curricular responsibilities such as information technology, special needs, or records of achievement, or administrative duties such as exams officer. These posts often held middle management status alongside the section heads. Some of them involved working in collaboration with colleagues who were themselves responsible for areas of the school's work, while others were largely administrative or involved working with a wide variety of staff in their teaching capacity.

THE CHARACTERISTICS OF MIDDLE MANAGEMENT POSTS

Heads were also asked to state the characteristics that defined middle management posts. Altogether, 254 different statements were made. Some identified very specific responsibilities of the particular post, which it was difficult to generalise from. Others were very vague statements such as 'head of department responsibility.' Many, however, identified precise yet general characteristics of middle management posts. It was possible to group the responses into 48 different characteristics, but thirty of these were mentioned only once, while four others were mentioned twice each: responsibility for exams administration, liaison with outside agencies, feeder schools and parents, liaison between the senior management team and assistant teachers, and the management of pupils. Five references were made to 'administration'.

Only seven groups of characteristics received more than ten references. The most common was responsibility for directing or co-ordinating the work of other teachers, sometimes expressed as 'management of staff', and sometimes referring to those staff as a 'team of teachers'. Altogether, 60 such statements were made. Within those 60, 14 references were made to the manager having responsibility for staff development as well. 42 references were made to having responsibility for, or being in charge of, a department, subject or pastoral unit of the school. In addition, another three made specific reference to the middle manager having responsibility for a faculty. These two basic characteristics – of responsibility for the work of other teachers and oversight and control of work in a defined area – were by far the most frequently mentioned. 25 heads referred to budgetary or resource control responsibilities, two writing in the language of cost centres, while 20 stated that a key characteristic was a line management relationship to a member of the senior management team, with accountability through that relationship for the standards of work achieved within their area of responsibility. This adds to the impression of the middle management task being one of control and delivery. By comparison, only 18 references were made to leadership, either of the teachers within a section of the school, or in relation to an area of work which was delivered through subjects but was defined as a separate responsibility, such as information technology or special needs. 17 references were made to the middle manager contributing in some way through an academic board, 'curriculum forum' or heads of department meeting to whole-school decision-making, while 15 referred to the middle manager as having cross-curricular responsibilities which would involve them in working with other managers rather than within their narrowly defined area. Only 6 heads wrote of middle managers being delegated considerable autonomy in their area of responsibility, although a small number referred to them taking decisions within their own area.

A number of points may be made in the light of these data. First, following on from our earlier discussion of the apparent division developing between 'B'/2 and 'D'/4 posts, it seems that the division we were suggesting between departmental and faculty, or year and 'school', as representing the point of entry into middle management does not hold. Most heads clearly saw any subject responsibility which involved organising the work of other teachers as having the status of middle management. This suggests that the majority of teachers in secondary schools will be regarded as middle management, and makes one wonder who the junior managers are!

A second point of importance is the language used when outlining the responsibilities of middle managers for the work of others. Although this was the most common aspect of the work, with 60 references being made to responsibilities for other staff, only 14 of these statements made any reference to staff development. Otherwise, the language used was that of co-ordination, direction and control. This indicates very clearly a view of middle managers as the faithful executors of policies handed down to them from senior staff. This is reflected in the small number of references to delegation and autonomy, although it is also clear that in some schools at least, middle managers were seen as having a useful input into wider school decision- and policy-making. It is also reflected in the way that leadership as a middle management task receives barely one-fifth of the references given to being in charge, co-ordination and direction.

We can conclude from these general statements that almost anyone with a promoted post in a secondary school with fewer than five responsibility points, or below the status of senior teacher, is likely to be seen as middle management, providing that they hold a defined responsibility area which involves them having to co-ordinate some aspect of the work of another teacher, and providing that they are not discharging these duties within what has traditionally been regarded as a single-subject department such as maths or English. It is not possible to differentiate between the expectations of a 'B' post and those of a 'C' or 'D' post in terms of the duties they must fulfil; the difference, if it exists, would appear to be in the size of the area of responsibility. It may be possible to confirm this by a closer examination of the job descriptions obtained.

THE DUTIES AND RESPONSIBILITIES OF PROMOTED POSTHOLDERS

1. The data in general terms

The detail and character of the job specifications received varied greatly, and this variation cut across all the levels of seniority, ranging from one sentence to over forty specific duties running to several pages. It was possible to analyse in detail 80 posts, distributed as follows:

	First survey	Second survey	Total number
'A' posts/1 allowance point	6	10	16
'B' posts/2 allowance points	18	22	40
'C' posts/3 allowance points	5	5	10
'D' posts/4 allowance points	7	7	14

The distribution of posts gives more representation to posts carrying 1–3 responsibility points than the national distribution reported above (Campbell and Neill 1991).

To help us compare the frequency with which a given duty was listed for different levels of post, we have calculated a mean score which divides the number of times a duty was cited in job descriptions by the number of posts paid at that level. Thus if there were 25 citations altogether of a particular responsibility, with 3 for 'A'/1 postholders, 6 for 'B'/2s, 6 for 'C'/3s and 10 for 'D'/4s, we would indicate these as 0.19 per 'A'/1 post (three citations against sixteen posts), 0.15 per 'B'/2 (six citations against forty posts), 0.3 per 'C'/3 (three against ten) and 0.71 per 'D'/4 (ten against fourteen). This particular distribution would suggest that the duty was more associated with more senior posts.

The average number of duties laid down for the posts analysed was 12.89. 'A'/1 point allowances averaged 8.56 duties and 'B'/2 posts 12.55, while 'C'/3 posts averaged 16.9 duties and 'D'/4 posts 15.92. This increase in administrative and managerial responsibilities is in line with the Campbell and Neill (1991) findings discussed above. Altogether 1,031 specific responsibilities were listed, which it was possible to organise into 169 different sets or categories of duties. We grouped these duties into eight broad areas of responsibility, and identified the frequency with which each area and category was cited, the distribution of categories across the areas of responsibility, and the importance of each area to each level of post, as shown by the frequency of citation. These figures are shown in Table 7.2.

We should be careful not to read too much into some of these figures, especially the less frequently cited areas of responsibility. In the case of external relations, for example, the figures are distorted by two modern languages posts among the 'A'/1s, and two music posts at the 'C'/3 level which

Table 7.2 Areas of responsibility, frequency of citation and distribution by seniority of post

Area of responsibility	No. of tasks cited	% of total citations	No. of categories of duty	% of total categories	Mean no. of citations per 'A'/1 post	Mean no. of citations per 'B'/2 post	Mean. no of citations per 'C'/3 post	Mean no. of citations per 'D'/4 post
Subject-related	242	23.5%	21	12.4%	2.19	3.18	3.4	3.29
Team/leadership/ interpersonal	205	19.9%	25	14.8%	1.0	2.73	3.3	3.36
Cross-curricular/ whole school	120	11.6%	29	17.1%	0.69	1.25	2.5	2.43
Assessment and records of achievement	103	10.0%	15	8.9%	0.69	1.5	1.9	0.93
Finance and resources	102	9.9%	18	10.6%	1.0	1.13	1.2	2.07
Teaching duties	90	8.7%	18	10.6%	1.94	0.93	1.2	0.78
External relations	64	6.2%	14	8.3%	0.69	0.5	2.2	0.79
Staff development, INSET and appraisal	62	6.0%	10	5.9%	0.25	0.8	0.6	1.43
Other administrative support	43	4.7%	19	11.2%	0.19	0.55	0.6	0.86

Source: Campbell and Neill 1991, p. 25.

were expected to promote a high profile for the school in the community through quality concerts and shows, and develop external sponsorship for the cultural and creative work of the school. In addition, the 'D'/4 result is inflated by the detailed specification of one Special Needs co-ordinator whose tasks involving external relations are itemised. Without that post, the mean score for 'D'/4 posts for external relations would have been 0.36 instead of 0.79.

We can note some clear trends. Subject-related duties are fairly consistent across all four levels, and assessment/records of achievement responsibilities are also consistently referred to except in 'A'/1 posts. Team-building, leadership and interpersonal skills become more important at 'C'/3 and 'D'/4 levels. There is a clear distinction over finance and resource responsibilities, these being much more common for 'D'/4 postholders. Cross-curricular and whole-school responsibilities are most commonly stated in the job descriptions for 'C'/3 and 'D'/4 posts. These differences stand at odds with the conclusions we drew from the heads' questionnaires, for they do suggest a distinction between 'A'/1 and 'B'/2 posts and those on higher allowances, with financial, leadership and interpersonal issues becoming more central to their work than for holders of lower paid jobs. We will explore this possible distinction as we look in more detail at the duties specified.

2. The detailed specification of duties

Of the total of 169 different duties and responsibilities identified within the 1,031 citations, 57 were mentioned only once, and another 22 only twice. 115 tasks were cited in job descriptions 5 times or fewer. By comparison, 3 were cited more than 30 times, and 14, 20 times or more. The 'top twenty' (actually 21) duties, cited 15 or more times, accounted for 47.4 per cent of the total (489 out of 1,031). Table 7.3 shows these tasks, the total number of citations, and the mean score per post analysed.

The distribution of these top twenty-one tasks reflects the overall frequency with which the areas of responsibility were cited. The two most frequently cited areas keep their places, and the next three, which had similar numbers of citations, remain together although financial tasks move up from fifth place to third. The area of staff development, INSET and appraisal also moves up, from eighth place to sixth. The 'top twenty' citations also count for a substantial percentage of all the areas of responsibility except for what has been called team/leadership/interpersonal, as Table 7.4 shows.

These figures suggest that we can define a core, albeit a relatively small one, of middle management responsibilities. It is, however, worth noting that around this core is a very large penumbra of idiosyncratic tasks, and it is important not to over-state the rationality of middle management responsibilities. The financial and cross-curricular areas, for example, both saw over one-quarter of all citations to tasks which were cited five times or less, and eighteen of the twenty-nine cross-curricular citations occurred only once. By comparison, the team/leadership/interpersonal area, although it

Table 7.3 The twenty-one most frequently cited duties for postholders in secondary schools

Task or duty	Area of responsibility	No. citations	Mean score
Create annual targets or schemes of work, or oversee and participate in this work	Subject-related	41	0.51
Advise, guide and support colleagues, maintain morale	Team/leadership/ interpersonal	35	0.44
Assist, or carry out as directed, curriculum planning or the development of teaching and learning strategies in line with national or local policies	Subject-related	33	0.41
Teach subject throughout school, or as directed	Teaching duties	28	0.35
Liaise with other schools or outside agencies, and/or secure service agreements	External relations	28	0.35
Supervise/oversee and co-ordinate colleagues' work, and ensure policies are followed through	Team/leadership/ interpersonal	26	0.33
Responsible for monitoring and controlling the use of stock and other resources in an area of responsibility	Finance/resources	25	0.31
Devise and monitor, or oversee pupil records in line with school, LEA or national policy	Assessment and records of achievement	25	0.31
Liaise with other staff concerning day-to-day activities or plans	Cross-curriculum/ whole school	24	0.3
Review and evaluate the curriculum/monitor teaching and learning and programme effectiveness	Subject-related	24	0.3
In charge of funds/resources for a department or faculty, including advising on budget share	Finance/resources	22	0.28
Co-ordinate, or be in charge of, a subject, year, or significant element of work agreed with head of faculty	Subject-related	22	0.28
In charge of curriculum development, implementation and evaluation in an area	Subject-related	21	0.26
Oversee or assist with the maintenance of fabric and facilities, including Health and Safety duties	Finance/resources	20	0.25
Represent the department to faculty or senior management and report back	Cross-curriculum/ whole school	18	0.23
Implement school policy within an area of responsibility	Subject-related	18	0.23
Co-ordinate and oversee assessment, marking and homework in line with school policies	Assessment and records of achievement	17	0.21
Collaborate in whole school/cross-curriculum planning	Cross-curriculum/ whole school	16	0.2
Prepare for and hold meetings and publish minutes	Team/leadership/ interpersonal	16	0.2
Keep abreast of developments and advise and inform colleagues	Staff development, INSET and appraisal	15	0.19
Devise and lead, or organise and publicise INSET	Staff development, INSET and appraisal	15	0.19

Table 7.4   Distribution of twenty-one most commonly cited secondary school tasks according to area of responsibility

Area of responsibility	Total tasks	Top twenty tasks	Total cited	Top twenty cited	Top twenty as % of total
Subject-related	21	6	242	159	65.7%
Team/leadership/ interpersonal	25	3	205	77	37.6%
Finance and resources	18	3	102	67	65.7%
Cross-curricular/ whole school	29	3	120	58	48.3%
Assessment and records of achievement	15	2	103	42	40.8%
Staff development, INSET and appraisal	10	2	62	30	48.4%
Teaching duties	18	1	90	28	31.1%
External relations	14	1	64	28	43.8%
Other administrative support	19	0	43	0	0

scored a low percentage of citations in the 'top twenty', saw the smallest percentage of any area scoring five citations or less.

The remainder of this section, then, is based mainly on the twenty-one most common citations, but also includes a broader look at the important area of interpersonal tasks.

The distribution of tasks between levels of seniority was not uniform, and it is possible to identify some as associated with 'D'/4 posts, while others are more commonly to be found among 'B'/2 posts. We can also differentiate in these more frequently cited duties between 'A'/1 posts and the rest. To do so, however, highlights the degree of confusion which exists in some heads' minds over who is to be regarded as 'middle management' and what their job is.

Taking first the subject-related tasks and duties, there was a clear difference between the seniority of posts which had responsibilities for creating annual targets and schemes of work or overseeing and participating in it, and those who were to assist in such activities. 'A'/1 postholders assisted, and 'B'/2 posts upwards created and exercised oversight. The scores for this were highest for 'D'/4 posts. Curriculum monitoring, evaluation and review were duties consistently allocated to all except 'A'/1 postholders, and 'B'/2 and 'C'/3 postholders appeared to shoulder the main responsibility for curriculum development in a subject area. 'A'/1 postholders were expected to co-ordinate a subject or an area of work, as were their senior colleagues below 'D'/4. The same distribution was to be found for the duty to implement school policy within a particular area.

This distribution suggests that in the field of subject-related duties the expectation of middle management is one of oversight and control, with faithful implementation of instructions below the 'C'/3 level finally giving way at the 'D'/4 to more oversight of others doing it.

In the area of responsibility which we called 'team, leadership and interpersonal', there was a clear rise with seniority in the extent to which a postholder was expected to advise, guide and support colleagues and sustain morale. This was far more commonly stated at the 'D'/4 level than at those below. Supervising and overseeing the work of others, however, was more complex, and appeared to be more important to more senior posts in 1991/2, but to move in location towards the 'B'/2 posts in 1994. This probably suggests that we should see it as something which is fairly consistently spread across the three more senior posts we are considering. However, we should not forget that the mean score for oversight was only 0.33, even though this was one of the higher mean scores recorded.

These responsibilities also produce a number of duties which were mentioned consistently but not frequently enough to figure in the 'top twenty'. A clutch of 'B'/2 posts were expected to support and deputise for their faculty head, and others, particularly 'B'/2s, had responsibility for overseeing ancillary staff. Some 'B'/2s and 'D'/4s were expected to arrange cover for absent colleagues, and 'A'/1 and 'B'/2 job descriptions sometimes enjoined their postholders to 'participate' as part of a team. It was interesting to find that leadership was rarely mentioned explicitly, and when it was, only as an activity which would result in the faithful implementation of school policies. This achieved a score of 0.18 for 'B'/2s, but received only one mention for each of the other three levels of post examined. Leadership, it seems, is not a middle management function at any level.

Financial responsibilities produced three of the most frequently cited tasks. The commonest, being in charge of stock, maintaining it and controlling its use, was consistently mentioned in all levels of seniority, although it appeared to be becoming more important at the 'A'/1 level over time. By comparison, responsibility for spending departmental or other funds was never afforded to 'A'/1 posts, and then increased in frequency as the posts became more senior, as was suggested at the end of the last section. Even then, however, it only reached a score of 0.5 for 'D'/4s, and for 'B'/2s, where it apparently increased in the frequency with which it was cited, it only reached a score of 0.38 in 1994.

The last task in this area of responsibility, that of overseeing and maintaining physical resources, was increasing in importance in the 1990s. Very few citations occurred in the first survey, and they were mainly at 'C'/3 or 'D'/4 levels, but they were in all levels of seniority by 1994.

Cross-curricular and whole-school tasks apparently decreased in importance between the two surveys. Liaison with colleagues over day-to-day activities remained important to 'B'/2 postholders, but disappeared from +3 and +4 posts, having scored above 0.6 for them two years before. In the same way, the task of representing a department or area to senior management and reporting back became even less significant for all levels. Whole-school planning remained exclusively in the world of 'C'/3 and 'D'/4 postholders, which confirms the impression suggested at the end of the previous section.

Perhaps surprisingly, tasks concerned with ensuring good assessment and record-keeping did not figure strongly, providing only two of the 'top twenty' tasks. An overall score of 0.31 was gained by tasks concerned with devising and monitoring the operation of a scheme of record-keeping in line with school, local authority or national policy, but these citations were concentrated mainly in the 'B'/2 posts. The task of co-ordinating and overseeing the operation of assessment and homework policies was low in the list (17th out of 21) and less important in 1994 than earlier. It was almost absent from 'A'/1 posts.

Tasks concerning staff development, in-service training and appraisal had a low and apparently declining priority. Even keeping up-to-date and informing one's colleagues of developments was rarely mentioned, scoring above 0.2 only for 'B'/2 and 'D'/4 posts. No reference was made to this in any special needs post, which was surprising. The decline was most pronounced in relation to in-service training: having been the fifth most frequently cited task in 1991/2, scoring 0.42 overall, it received no citations in 1994. In 1991/2, however, it was clearly seen as important at both the 'B' and 'D' levels.

The last two areas of responsibility show completely the reverse pattern. Teaching responsibilities were mentioned frequently in 'A'/1 posts, occasionally in 'B'/2s but hardly at all in the others. External liaison was exclusively a 'C'/3 and 'D'/4 responsibility.

3. The implications of these job descriptions for the middle management role

We can summarise the key elements of these posts into four sets of responsibilities: for curriculum, for the work of others, for contributing to whole-school activities, and for finance and resources. The third and fourth elements were more limited in their applicability, being limited in the main to more senior posts. There was a clear culture in the language of the job descriptions that the postholders would be in charge of delivering what was laid down rather than involved in developing what was to be done, overseeing and ordering what their teams did rather than developing the work in a constructive or collaborative way. There was little reference to leadership and development, almost none to motivating and encouraging staff, and much to organising and implementing. The curricular duties laid down referred repeatedly to laying down or planning the annual schemes of work, but the way in which this was expressed suggested that these were to be the day-to-day realisation of given and non-negotiable curricula. A similar culture of control and direction was present in the references to duties in the area of assessment and records of achievement.

There was also a small but significant element of ensuring that the right teaching methods and approaches were employed. 'A' and 'B' posts referred repeatedly to *assisting* in curriculum planning and development, which suggested a difference in the range of responsibility and autonomy between these posts and those paid on 'C' and 'D' allowances.

Collegial and collaborative approaches to departmental or unit management were rarely mentioned, notwithstanding the frequency with which lower posts were required to 'assist'. This assistance is apparently to be given on the head of unit's terms, as some of the responsibilities listed under 'other administrative support', but not discussed in detail here, confirm.

One obvious reason why the more highly paid posts may have more emphasis on team responsibilities is that the number of people in the units for which they are responsible is likely to be greater. However, as was suggested above, and as the relatively high importance which 'A' post job descriptions attached to giving advice to colleagues acknowledges, a teacher who has responsibility for a small area of work but who has to rely on colleagues providing some teaching time on the margins of their main commitment has a task which may be as difficult as leading a team of several full-time teachers.

Contributions to whole-school planning and curricular decision-making were limited, for the most part, to 'D' postholders, but stood somewhat uneasily alongside the language of faithful implementation of what was required. There was an element of 'representing the interests of your section' in these duties, but for the most part it was a question more of contributing information which could then be worked over by the senior management. There was little evidence that the academic board, 'curriculum forum' or heads of department/head of year meetings were decision-making bodies. The participation of these most highly paid middle managers appeared to be limited to suggestion and comment. It was also striking that very few job descriptions spoke of attempting to generate on-the-ground collaboration between departments or administrative units of the school.

Financial responsibility was also largely limited to the most senior jobs analysed, with more junior posts being limited to forms of resource and stock control. It was rarely explained how the budgets for sub-units were decided, so it seems, again, that the responsibility is largely one of dealing with what is laid down as efficiently and effectively as possible, rather than trying to influence what is laid down.

There is, then, considerable evidence of a difference between 'B'/2 posts and 'D'/4 posts. The status of 'C'/3 posts is no clearer at the end of this survey than it was before, but they may be a combination of 'D'/4 posts which are currently underpaid because of lack of resources and 'B'/2 departments which are small in terms of the number of staff involved but which have high profile work within the school, such as music or, in a denominational school, RE. Some special needs posts in smaller schools appeared to qualify for three responsibility points on both counts! However, the lack of a clear hierarchical relationship between the 'B'/2 and 'D'/4 posts in many cases makes it difficult to state that 'B'/2 should no longer be seen as a middle management position, although it may be that we are moving in that direction. We shall continue, somewhat reluctantly, to regard 'B'/2 to 'D'/4 posts as the middle management level in schools, even though many 'B'/2s have spans of responsibility which in other settings would have them regarded as junior management or even supervisory grade.

Activity 7.3
How closely does the analysis in this chapter, and the conclusion just offered, match the situation in your school? You should consider this question from three points of view:
- that of the headteacher as expressed in job descriptions and organisational charts;
- that of your colleagues in your area of responsibility; and
- that of the postholders with responsibility areas, viewed as a collectivity.

It is also worth commenting that there appeared to be evidence of a difference between 'A'/1 posts and the others. Their job descriptions placed a far stronger emphasis on teaching responsibilities than the others did, but also appeared to give more emphasis to ensuring that they offered advice to others on their area of responsibility. It may be that this was seen as advice within the department or faculty rather than within the wider school setting, but the tenor of the 'A'/1 post job descriptions suggested that the posts were seen as training positions rather than substantive management responsibilities. This would be in line with the comment in some headteacher responses to the questionnaire that 'A'/1 posts were largely if not entirely temporary positions for people working on particular short-term projects, often within working parties.

This view of the data suggests that postholders carrying fewer than five responsibility points hold limited responsibilities in a very fragmented and sectionalised school system. This is held together by the overview provided by senior management teams, and they play little part in influencing this overview. This perception is supported by Glover's (1994) review of Ofsted reports on secondary schools. The main findings and key issues for action repeatedly make statements suggesting that 'middle management' is cut off from whole-school decisions, particularly those concerned with longer-term planning, even when faculty and departmental planning is deemed 'effective'. There is a clear, rational assumption that middle managers should be participants in the school's policy-making process, that this should rest upon good information, and that institutional and unit development plans should be in step with one another.

Glover also provides evidence to suggest that Ofsted regard the obligations of departmental managers in a rather different light from our job descriptions. Curriculum planning is declared to be important, but this needs to take account of both content obligations and the need for continuity and differentiation. Surprisingly, perhaps, these are not much discussed in the job specifications we have studied, although examples are to be found. Well-run departments, according to Ofsted, are not just concerned with the day-to-day, but have medium-term development plans which link resources to actions. This idea is almost entirely absent from job descriptions and headteacher questionnaires, where the extent of planning is limited to the annual schemes of work. Ofsted inspectors made more of issues of assessment, resource-allocation and monitoring, and team-building than our job specifications have done, and placed considerable emphasis on monitoring and evaluating practice, which suggests that this expectation in the job descriptions is not being acted upon.

This suggests that the issues of subcultural fragmentation which were discussed earlier may be significant, since the whole-school perspective is less significant for the middle manager than delivering what is required within the department, even though Ofsted is trying to encourage senior staff to draw them into wider planning concerns. Heads of department or faculty may therefore have to reconcile the demands of requirements placed upon them with the beliefs and expectations of their colleagues. It also suggests that heads of department, faculty, and pastoral units may not be able to meet the demands of their posts in uniform ways: they need to pay more attention to the immediate circumstances in which they have to carry out their work. While it may be possible to generate some basic principles to take into account when planning and thinking about their work, actually carrying it out is likely to be much more messy than the purveyors of what one might call 'cookery-book management' like to suggest.

8

Secondary School Middle Management in Action: Some Case Studies

As well as formal expectations, managers are affected in their work by their personal values and assumptions which influence their interpretations of those expectations and of the organisation they work in. Case studies can demonstrate this, and we shall consider six now: two heads of science from different schools, followed by three heads of department from within the same school. Lastly a head of maths considers the impact of school restructuring on her role after the school became grant maintained. The cases were all prepared between 1988 and 1995; the older ones were checked for relevance by practising departmental heads during the 1994/5 school year. All the names, of course, have been changed.

As with the primary case studies, there are no activities in this chapter. However, I suggest that as you read each case study you bear in mind the following questions:

- What similarities can I identify between this person's situation and my own in terms of school setting, department or 'basic unit' culture, my management responsibilities, and colleagues' expectations and attitudes?
- In what ways does the case differ from my situation?
- How similar is my view of my management responsibilities (or those I hope soon to hold) to that of this case study subject?
- Where there are particular activities or events described in the case study, would I have done them differently in my school? If so, why?

At the end of each case, you should ask yourself:

- What does this case study teach me about my approach to management responsibilities, and about the expectations of my colleagues and senior management? What changes or re-appraisals ought I to consider to my practice?

CASE STUDY 1: HEAD OF SCIENCE EUAN CAMPBELL

Euan Campbell had been head of physics at Albemarle Park School for three years before becoming head of science in the term before he was interviewed. It was his third school. When he began teaching, he set himself the target of being a head of department within five years: he made it in six. He also decided to exploit the physics side of his degree in preference to others which he had enjoyed more because physics was a shortage area at the time. Having achieved head of physics, he had realised that his ambitions ran higher, although they stopped short of headship because he saw himself as an organiser rather than a public relations specialist, which was how he saw headship. He enjoyed management and organisation, which included motivating colleagues, and said he was good at it; sometimes, indeed, he enjoyed it more than teaching.

He said that there was a lot needing attention within his department but it could not be put right overnight: change in education should be an evolutionary rather than revolutionary process, even when outside agencies are imposing major and rapid change. Thus he saw his role as involving buffering his department from unnecessary change and controlling what was going on within it to ensure that what was required was what was happening, although the decisions upon which the activities were based may not have been entirely his own.

His department of six full-time teachers and two part-timers, along with three technicians, was experienced and stable. The teachers included two ex-heads of science, one of whom had been in post for sixteen years before becoming head of lower school, while the other, actually head of chemistry, held the more senior post for a year before Euan was appointed. The head also taught in the department. In addition, the teacher in charge of biology, a standard scale teacher, had joined the school as a probationary teacher ten years before. There was little collaboration or co-operation: the teacher in charge of biology said he had been left to sink or swim, and only when Euan arrived had anyone joined the department who would offer helpful advice.

Euan said he was responsible for the 'day-to-day management of that group of people, with the personality problems that many face'. Motivation was a key problem: some staff were nearing retirement, and saw external decisions destroying much of what they had stood for, while others felt barred from promotion or unable to contribute positively to the department because of how it had run in the past. He realised that his own views were quite different from some of the senior staff who taught science, and so he faced what he saw as the problem of changing viewpoints and creating a new teaching framework without provoking confrontation. Staff development could help with this, but he said that the problems were so great that this would have to wait.

He also acknowledged technical responsibilities: oversight of the five science laboratories and three preparation rooms, responsibility for equipment and consumable resources, including the chemical store, and record-keeping. These, too, had been inadequately dealt with before his appointment. Health and Safety legislation had to be observed, which involved knowing what his teaching and ancillary colleagues were doing: they could not be allowed to operate as they saw fit.

As well as these internal responsibilities, Euan acknowledged some school-wide duties, notably to support academic development and academic committees, parental meetings and other major events designed to demonstrate the quality of education provided. However, his first duty was to get his department into shape. Within his subject area of physics, in which he was the only specialist, he was able to exploit the specialist and objectivist epistemology discussed earlier: he taught most of the physics in years ten and above, including all the A-level work, and controlled the rest through schemes of work for the year and end-of-year examinations. The laboratory technician was a key figure here: by setting out the same equipment for the experiments as Euan had used or specified, the technician could limit the freedom of action available to the teachers, while leaving their approach to teaching and explaining the experiment for them to decide. However, Euan was always ready to discuss the course and its teaching. Monitoring external examination courses was more difficult because teachers resisted the idea of being observed and there was in any case little opportunity to do it, but he exploited the annual inquest on exam results and used departmental progress-tests. He looked at exercise books and checked that proper homeworks were being set and marked, another area of weakness which he had identified within the department.

Euan was also keen to involve colleagues more in decisions on what should be taught and how. He saw it as crucial to recognise others' expertise, since otherwise he would not be making the most of his colleagues, so he was keen to have them raise issues and make suggestions. However, although he was concerned not to dictate, he believed he was responsible for taking the final decisions on what teaching arrangements and schemes of work were to operate in the department, rather than the individual subject heads who in practice made these decisions. He was finding this sort of involvement hard to generate, since, as he put it, the teachers had all spent so long in the school. Consequently, responses were negative – 'we've tried it before and it doesn't work.' This led him towards more subtle strategies, attempting to sell ideas informally which then reappeared as someone else's suggestion that he could take up and encourage the department to adopt.

This strategy could work in other settings: he used it to persuade the headteacher to ask him to require the former head of science to make teaching his exam classes take priority over dealing with pastoral matters associated with his new post, a move which was necessary since the teacher concerned saw himself as senior to Euan.

Euan Campbell, then, was concerned mainly with persuading the science teachers to agree to and implement a particular pattern of relationships and responsibilities, and ensuring that their teaching was in line both with the schemes of work and with one another's practice. However, as well as this internal reform, he also saw himself as needing to defend his department if necessary. He stated that he would not hesitate to take a matter to a higher authority should it seem necessary, including if necessary going above the headteacher, something he had done in his previous career in social work.

Euan's department was insular and stale, and he wanted to change this. His rationalist, objectivist epistemology led him to approach this through shaping the teaching of his colleagues, and his assumptive world or theory in use allowed him to see his role as combining leadership with control. He would defend his 'patch' and those who worked within it, providing they gave him what he was asking for in return, but he also sought to create clear limits to the kinds of involvement he wished to promote. Thus the discussion he wished to see would not be a collegial decision-making approach to science department policy, but taking soundings and gathering ideas and experience upon which he could base the final decision.

CASE STUDY 2: HEAD OF SCIENCE HENRY ASHTON

Henry Ashton had also worked outside schools before becoming a teacher, as a research chemist and in publishing. He became a head of department within three years of entering teaching, and had been a head of science at the St Thomas More School for seven years when he was interviewed. Thus he had more experience at the senior level than Euan Campbell.

Like Euan, Henry Ashton had responsibility for six other staff and three technicians, and he also cited Health and Safety responsibilities and resource allocation. He said that he was responsible for deciding which syllabuses and courses to follow, for setting work for cover lessons if necessary, and, should the teacher be absent for any length of time, marking that work. In addition, St Thomas More was a very tightly staffed school with some poor attenders, so Henry frequently lost all his non-contact time in a week to cover lessons.

Henry also acknowledged responsibility for staff development, although he felt to some extent inadequate to deal with this. One science teacher had a very bad attendance record, with regular absences every week which appeared to be related to her teaching duties. He felt that she needed counselling and support which he was unable to provide. Consequently, he believed that senior staff should take on such a problem, and it was not happening.

Henry's department was experiencing high and rapid turnover as a succession of young teachers came and gained rapid promotion outside. Consequently, he felt obliged to take responsibility for determining the scheme of work and writing the worksheets and detailed lesson plans for much of the science teaching in the school. He estimated that some 80 per cent of the worksheets and plans in use in the department were his, although they were starting to replace some of these with commercial materials when we spoke. In part he had taken responsibility for preparing the programme because of a fundamental disagreement between himself and his second in department (an unsuccessful internal candidate for the job, who had continued at the school for four years after Henry came) over the proper relationship between single subject and 'balanced' science, with Henry being a strong advocate of the balanced science now enshrined in the national curriculum. He stated that he had been appointed specifically to implement balanced science, and the newly appointed headteacher had helped him to do this quickly, but in the absence at that time of satisfactory commercial materials it had been necessary to produce their own.

His worksheets were very prescriptive as to objectives, content and outcomes. For example, the data from an experiment might have to be presented in a particular graphical form. However, he did not specify in detail, lesson by lesson, exactly what approach the teachers should be taking. He always offered a list of recommended practicals, but also said that he did not feel entitled to insist on any teacher using a practical they felt unable to use.

However, in other ways he was extremely prescriptive, which was why he would not share the work of constructing the worksheets and programmes of study as extensively as he might have done: teachers in their first year, or inexperienced in an area or level of teaching, needed to be told what they were to do. Further, he monitored their work to ensure that they were following instructions, by looking at exercise books and lesson plans, examining the marks they had given, and when possible observing them in action.

Such observation was made easier by the physical layout of the science laboratories, which Henry described as 'a set of corridors between store cupboards'. Consequently, people were always passing through each others' classes, so much informal observation occurred. Henry indicated that this was normal in his experience of science departments and that he would act to prevent any particular individual becoming the teacher who worked in 'the lab. at the end of the corridor'. His sense that science teachers were usually at ease with such informal movement through others' classrooms was strengthened by the attitudes expressed elsewhere in the research from which this case was drawn.

Informal observation tended to result in informal comments later, often of a helpful and supportive nature ('I liked that diagram of . . .'). This was one factor which generated a cohesive and supportive department into which young, upwardly mobile teachers could fit comfortably. It also made it easier for the teams of staff teaching particular year-groups to meet to review progress, amend schemes for the following year, and plan the next stage together. This had been especially important when GCSE had been introduced, since there were no guidance notes or specimen assessment papers, and teachers were thrown on to their own resources in preparing the first groups of pupils for the exams. However, such collegiality was limited to teachers collectively working out how to fulfil instructions, not to deciding what to do.

Although he had been in post for six years, Henry made no reference to any school-wide responsibilities as head of science. He described the school as a difficult environment with a divided and carping staff, an unpopular head (at least with the older, longer-established staff), and some very unpopular senior staff appointments. His response was to retreat into his departmental responsibilities and only use school-wide networks if it was absolutely essential. For example, he rarely used the pastoral system, feeling that the staff were inadequate and that any acknowledgement of problems led to derision as a 'failure' from some teachers. Consequently he, and other teachers, guarded their own backs carefully from such criticism.

Henry Ashton's view of his job was in many ways similar to Euan Campbell's. It involved major responsibility for determining and ensuring satisfactory delivery of a curriculum in line with mandated requirements or senior staff policies, and for ensuring that relevant standards of assessment and classroom/laboratory practice were maintained. Both of these heads of science were operating as agents of higher authority, with clear directive and control functions. The main difference between the two lies in their attitude towards the wider school context. Euan Campbell saw this in a positive light, while at the same time claiming that it was necessary to manipulate others in the interests of the department, while Henry Ashton saw it in a negative light, and saw his main responsibility as being a protective one, not just for the interests of the department as a unit, but also for his staff.

Thus our middle manager heads of science had much in common. They were a mixture of bureaucratic and political managers, recognising and exercising control functions and seeing themselves as responsible for implementing curricular policy decisions which were taken at senior levels but which they made operational. One saw himself as having an input into such decisions; the other, as having been appointed because he was in sympathy with it. They saw themselves as exercising control in similar ways, made acceptable by the objectivist epistemology of a department of specialist subject teachers. However, one wished to influence a potentially supportive wider environment while the other felt he had to defend his department against it. Two different departments in different institutional cultures and settings, but dealing with the same area of responsibility, have strong similarities. When we turn to considering middle managers with different areas of responsibility in the same school, and therefore operating in the same institutional culture and setting, we find far stronger differences between them. The school involved, Sarah Lawley School for girls, was a five-form-entry 11–18 comprehensive school of just over 800 pupils and 50 staff. It shared a campus with the equivalent boys' school (there was only one of each in the borough) but except for the TVEI scheme which had been created there was no collaboration between the schools.

CASE STUDY 3: HEAD OF YEAR ELEVEN AND HEAD OF HISTORY BARRY REYNOLDS

Barry Reynolds had come to Sarah Lawley eight years before becoming head of history, and had been appointed to what is now head of year eleven three years later. He saw them as quite distinct, and so we will consider them separately.

He said he was simply the co-ordinator of the teachers of history, because the others were so experienced: a deputy head, who was an ex-head of history, a 'D' allowance holder and ex-head of history but now with other responsibilities, a head of year, and a retired ex-headteacher on a part-time contract. Faced with this array of experience and expertise, Barry felt he had little direction or control to exercise! Thus the last departmental meeting had involved allocating various tasks for people to carry out and sharing information about how the girls were answering particular kinds of questions in the mock GCSE exam paper. His view of curriculum development was one of chairing discussions and giving an initial lead, but not of directing it in a particular way.

His approach to innovation, which he saw as a key responsibility, was conditioned by the internal relations within the department, which were very open: it was quite acceptable to enter a colleague's class to go to the stock cupboard, and such a visit would often result in being drawn into the lesson ('I wonder what Mr Reynolds thinks about this?'). Consequently, although the staff did not teach in a uniform way, or as a team, they knew one another's approaches and their strengths and weaknesses. One member of staff was always ready to try new ideas, and the others were always keen to try them out themselves if they were seen as useful, bearing in mind their own knowledge of the teacher concerned and their own teaching approaches. Indeed, Barry viewed this teacher as a major element in his own professional development, and thought himself a more confident and less conservative teacher as a result. For him, then, the department was as important a source of leadership and ideas to influence his own work as he was a source of leadership to them.

Even so, and perhaps because they were themselves all successful senior teachers, the other staff appeared to be more ready to follow Barry's lead than he was sometimes ready for. Certainly prior to the national curriculum he had prepared a lesson-by-lesson syllabus for the lower school which incorporated core lessons which had to be taught and options which the teachers could use, develop or ignore as they saw fit. He had worried over doing this, but after a debate as to the proper nature of the syllabus the staff apparently actively encouraged the idea and supported it in their teaching.

Although monitoring the work of others in his department was a designated responsibility, he found it very difficult to do formally, and relied instead on what he knew from his informal visits to others' classrooms. He also said that the other teachers were open about their marking practices, and that departmental meetings provided a lot of information about what was happening – for example, discussions at a departmental meeting about what should be set in a lower school exam had revealed the need for a more directive syllabus. The fact that departmental members felt confident enough to acknowledge error or failure in the sense of an unsuccessful approach to a topic or lesson made direct monitoring less important.

Barry believed that one major reason why the department exchanged ideas so freely and developed such a relaxed attitude to other teachers interrupting their classroom work was that they tended to congregate in his office, where there was a coffee-maker and a stereo unit. Because all of them had other duties which kept them busy at break times, they were relatively rarely in the staffroom and saw a lot more of each other than they did of the rest of the staff.

Overall, then, there was a professionally constructed consensus which derived from the high level of competence and experience among the departmental members, allied to their all holding senior office in the school, enabling the head of history to operate as a co-ordinator rather than director. His style of management was a complex collegiality in which officeholders who were confident of their skill as teachers of history worked together while acknowledging an ultimate authority in one particular office. It was not clear what would have happened to this view of one another had one member of the department been found wanting, or if Barry's view of good practice in history teaching had been at odds with the others'. The fact that it was not made a relaxed, non-directive perception of his role possible, even though he was allowed to exercise far more direction than he acknowledged.

Barry also had wider responsibilities. As a head of department, he attended a regular cycle of heads' of department meetings, there being no faculty system at the school. These were frustrating, because he found that they focused on what he regarded as trivia rather than substantive issues: how many girls were wearing the right kind of pullover rather than matters of curriculum policy. In this wider arena, he felt that it was appropriate to exercise the authority of office: heads of department were the major authorities on the curriculum, and because of their knowledge power, they should have a major part to play in generating decisions on curriculum planning, development and evaluation.

Barry saw his role as a head of year as more difficult to deliver. Essentially it was a supportive role for both teachers and pupils: it was his job to identify areas of concern and then to find the best means of dealing with them, and the school had laid down procedures for passing on information about problems to the pastoral team which, if followed, would allow for this to happen. But teachers were often reluctant to pass on this information, especially if it concerned disciplinary problems. Although the school staffroom was generally supportive and open, with informal discussions on educational matters going on between a core of staff long after the school day had ended, difficulties acknowledged informally to friends in the staffroom were not passed on to the staff who had the authority and responsibility to assist in a more formal way.

The contrast between the successful and relaxed departmental side of Barry's managerial work and his struggle to deliver the kind of managerial support which he felt was his responsibility as a head of year is striking. He saw the management function as one of supporting and enabling a team of people to work together effectively, and was reluctant to exercise a control or command function. However, his view of his role as a head of year asked his colleagues to acknowledge weaknesses, and the culture of Sarah Lawley did not allow that easily. At St Thomas More school, the deputy head (pastoral) stated clearly that such support and assistance was a departmental responsibility, with the pastoral care side being responsible for developing and delivering a formal pastoral curriculum.

Barry Reynolds' experience as head of history and head of year shows how we must take account of both the character, status and experience of the people over whom we have managerial authority and what we have to require of them in order to carry out our view of our work effectively. In this, a key issue is the question of trust. Barry Reynolds' subject department trusted him, and trusted each other. Consequently, it worked collaboratively together. As head of year, on the other hand, he needed information which staff were often reluctant to give, for fear of the consequences for their own professional status within the school. The issue of trust is a major one to be addressed by any manager, and we shall encounter it again.

CASE STUDY 4: HEAD OF HOME ECONOMICS ANDREA HACKETT

The case of Andrea Hackett may seem old-fashioned, since it rests on interview data collected before the national curriculum proposals had been published. However, it is instructive because of the assumptions she made about her work and how it should be done. They are still common among some teachers, in their relations both with colleagues and with their pupils.

Andrea Hackett was head of home economics and teacher with responsibility for equal opportunities within the TVEI scheme, on the equivalent of four responsibility points. She had taken up the post four years earlier, having come from an FE college where she had been a lecturer with a responsibility area in the hotel and catering department. Her experience in the FE college, where she felt she was the only 'educational professional' among a group of male 'catering professionals', had made her determined to change home economics into the study of food and nutrition rather than 'buns and cakes, and more buns and more cakes'. She was told on her appointment by the previous headteacher that she was expected to bring about that change.

Before she formally took up her post, Andrea analysed the department's syllabus from the point of view of a group of HE teachers who had developed a clear philosophy and approach, and whom she had met through in-service courses. She prepared a completely new course for the incoming year seven, but for the rest she attempted to combine the best of the old with the central elements of what she wanted. This failed for two reasons. First, both of her colleagues were strongly opposed to the changes. Andrea felt that their attitude to their work was unprofessional. Second, the two philosophies were so totally at odds that they could not be married together: after a month even her colleagues were saying that it would be better to adopt the new course wholesale. She recognised that carrying through total change effectively told the other teachers that everything they had ever taught was wrong, and was bound to generate a sense of inadequacy in the teachers in her department, but declared that they should not have got so out-of-date, so their fate was 'just tough'. Both the teachers left within the year.

Andrea described her approach to this reform as negotiation. Colleagues had to report to departmental meetings on what they had done, and how well it had gone, and problems were then discussed. Thus it became clear that her reform programme had to be root-and-branch. It also enabled her to win all the arguments against her approach, so that ultimately both her colleagues resigned.

The two teachers who left were replaced by two probationary teachers. One had been trained at the college where Andrea had done her own in-service B.Ed and therefore held the same philosophy; the other was more traditional, but easier to influence than a more experienced teacher might have been.

The new syllabus she introduced was very tightly prescribed, with clear objectives for each lesson expressed in terms of specific skills. She argued that prior specification was preferable to the *ad hoc* approach which had previously been taken, and did not accept that it would prevent spontaneity. Departmental meetings were used to discuss difficulties being experienced. Having previously been the vehicle for demonstrating to the former teachers how inadequate their methods, approach and syllabus all were, they now became the means by which Andrea monitored practice. However, she believed that observing her colleagues in the classroom was unprofessional, since it usurped their authority, so she would not go into a classroom even to help a colleague. Instead, she said, she would 'chat' about what had happened, and reminisce about problems of a similar sort she had faced.

Andrea was hostile to much of her school environment, and appeared to run home economics as a largely separate entity. From the outset she had refused to continue to provide the catering for school functions, thus challenging the authoritarian previous head who, she said, ran the school 'like a military academy'. Although the school was more open under its current head, she still used the pastoral system purely as a vehicle for passing information, and refused 'to waste ten minutes in every lesson dealing with rings and make-up'.

However, in the field of equal opportunities she insisted that the school established formal policies and policed them. This would enable her to pressure both senior and junior staff, and was, she believed, the only way to deal with people who were very resistant to change.

Andrea Hackett came across as a very authoritarian head of department, accepting a brief and imposing it come what may, but interpreting it according to her own philosophy. She clearly felt that she had the authority to prepare and implement a completely new programme and philosophy of home economics teaching, and that the scale and direction of the changes in her department were entirely at her discretion. She presented her approach to change as what Bennis, Benne and Chin (1985) called 'empirical-rational', demonstrating through force of argument that what she wanted was best and persuading her colleagues to agree, but it came across in interview as essentially 'power-coercive', forcing her colleagues to discuss what they were doing, to acknowledge difficulties and problems, and then telling them how to deal with them. This authoritarianism came through again in her wish to use policy statements to pressure other staff. Yet she was quick to reserve to herself the right to ignore any school policy directives she disliked.

The overwhelming impression Andrea Hackett created was of a manager who did not trust her colleagues and sought ways of reducing their discretion while maximising her own. Policy directives and tightly prescriptive syllabuses, with regular meetings at which staff had to report on their progress, limited the extent to which individual teachers would be able to interpret policies in their own way and in the light of circumstances and their own theories in use or assumptive worlds. Although she presented herself as an advocate of teacher professionalism, in practice she attempted to force her departmental colleagues to do only what they were told. There was no sense of trusting her colleagues or building a sense of a team philosophy or spirit, nor of generating leadership responsibilities or opportunities for her colleagues, and no sense either of a group of teachers working harmoniously together in a collegium.

CASE STUDY 5: HEAD OF ENGLISH WENDY EDWARDS

Wendy Edwards had been a head of English for most of her twenty-plus years of teaching prior to moving to her present post. However, this was her first post in a comprehensive school, a move she had made because she had always felt guilty about not living out her socialist principles, and because in the head of the school she felt there was a supportive colleague whom she could trust if she needed help.

She said she was responsible for the teaching of English throughout the school: for the syllabus, for resources, and for providing assistance as necessary to departmental colleagues. She was diffident about giving direction, especially in matters of teaching and control, since her move to a comprehensive had presented her with problems she had not met since she was a probationer. She also recognised that it had been easy for English teachers to adapt programmes or syllabuses and take little notice of them, although this was less straightforward since the introduction of the national curriculum and testing at key stage 3. Because English teachers could ignore instructions and syllabuses so easily, she believed that she had to involve her colleagues in writing syllabuses and schemes of work, since only by gaining their involvement in planning and preparation could she hope to gain their commitment to implementing the results.

Circumstances had helped her to promote this position in which collaboration was seen as desirable but she was not expected to direct. Prior to her arrival, the English department had been a fragmented and unco-operative group of teachers, in which personal experience was the only acknowledged basis for deciding what to do in a given situation. Immediately upon her appointment she had to deal with the introduction of GCSE and thereafter with all the problems of the national curriculum. GCSE had been a godsend, since it levelled all the teachers into a situation of apparent ignorance which left her own uncertainty about teaching in a comprehensive less of a disadvantage: since no one had taught GCSE before, who could advise anyone else on the basis of their experience of teaching it? This situation more or less forced the department to collaborate, and she commented approvingly on the impact of one training day which had demonstrated clearly how it was essential for the teachers in a year-group to plan a programme and its implementation, and then stick to what had been planned.

This pressure had made the development of good personal relations within the department a priority for her. Collaboration and co-operation, she said, depended on developing trust between the staff, and as the head of department she had to ensure that all her colleagues trusted her. Fortnightly departmental meetings alone were inadequate for this, so Wendy took every opportunity she could for informal conversations. She believed that liking one another was a precondition of trust, so set out deliberately to help her colleagues feel that she valued their work and liked them. Good relations, she said, followed naturally.

She was helped to develop this new departmental culture by the presence of a recently deployed young teacher. The two women had very different strengths: while the head of department was strong on literature and content knowledge, her colleague seemed, in Wendy's words, never to have any discipline problems and was a potential source of useful advice. They found they could ask each other for advice, and this became a way of leading by example, since as they developed in confidence they continued to discuss ideas and problems. Working together with her colleague in this way strengthened Wendy's attempts to generate more collective decision-making and support.

One demonstration of this growing support for each other within the department was the policy they established for dealing with difficult or disruptive students. If a teacher felt that one or two girls' behaviour was seriously holding back the rest of the class, they would ask if someone else would take the problems for a week so that the rest of the class could get on with some uninterrupted work. (This was possible, of course, because of blocked timetabling.) No one felt that this was admitting 'failure', since everyone had done it, including the head of department, and it meant that most serious discipline problems could be contained within the department, with the pastoral system simply being kept informed. However, it was at the request of the teacher, not on the head of department's initiative, and Wendy felt this was important.

The contrast between Wendy Edwards and Andrea Hackett as managers is summed up in their approach to managing change. Andrea believed she had to establish the purity of her ideology and philosophy of teaching home economics. She drove out the two older teachers who disagreed, replacing them with probationers who either shared that philosophy or would do as they were told. She laid down a clear and tightly prescribed syllabus and reviewed progress publicly every fortnight at departmental meetings. She believed that her approach was a rational one, in which every argument that was put up against her beliefs was shot down so that there was no alternative to following what she wanted. No emphasis was placed on interpersonal relationships or the development of teams or co-operative working: the job of home economics teachers was to do what they were told.

Wendy disagreed. Partly because of the tradition of autonomous teaching within English, and partly because she was uncertain if she could cope in a comprehensive school, she felt unable to direct and require in the same way. Further, she did not believe that she should do so. Consequently, although she too had her own ideas about what the English teaching in her department should look like, she could only bring this about by first causing a cultural change in the department, so that people would move from a sense of being valued to trusting their head of department, and thence to being prepared to co-operate in planning and implementing a revised syllabus. As it happened, the introduction of GCSE and then the national curriculum created an external climate in which co-operation, reassurance and a need to sense that they were valued for what they did all became necessary for her departmental colleagues to keep going, and it was clear that the English department did sustain its activity effectively through the reforms.

CASE STUDY 6: CO-ORDINATOR OF MATHEMATICS CHRISTINE URQUHART

Christine Urquhart was co-ordinator of mathematics at Morland High School, a mixed suburban comprehensive of 1,000 pupils and 62 staff. This post was created in the school's restructuring when it became grant maintained nine months before our interview: previously she had been head of maths for six years. She had taught at the school for fourteen years.

Much of her job specification remained unchanged by the restructuring. She had to oversee the production of schemes of work by colleagues, allocate resources and teachers, and ensure that all assessments and reports were completed satisfactorily and on schedule. She had overall responsibility for the maths budget, which she separated from resource management, and was the first line of referral for staff when they experienced discipline problems. The new development with the changed job title was that she was expected to represent the department to higher committees in the school, particularly through the newly established fortnightly meetings of the eight curriculum co-ordinators.

Christine was uneasy about the idea that she should monitor her colleagues' teaching. In practice, she believed she exercised responsibility for maths teaching by monitoring assessments and reports. However, this was adequate because the department had been very stable: apart from a new appointment to take up the newly created second-in-department post the previous September, there had been no change of staff for some years. They shared a common view of education and of teaching approaches in mathematics, and also agreed on the extent of their commitment to the school. She described the department as 'close' and said they 'look after one another'.

Because they shared a common outlook and the exam results were satisfactory, Christine did not attempt to investigate her colleagues' work in detail. Nor did she want to prescribe teaching approaches: she said she wanted teachers in the department, not robots. She had a fair idea of what took place, because they shared an adjacent suite of rooms, and her office was there, so although the classroom doors stayed firmly closed she was aware of most problems that arose. However, she recognised that it would be very difficult to challenge the established practice of a colleague if problems emerged, and she would find it hard to investigate another teacher's classroom practice in detail. She would rely on exercise books and what the pupils said, and would ask the individual concerned what they did in teaching particular topics. She was also prepared to observe classes, but had not had to do so.

Christine, then, ran a cohesive and supportive department on the basis of a shared philosophy of maths teaching and confidence in one another's teaching ability so that monitoring by outcomes alone was sufficient. She recognised that she was 'inclined to be bossy', so worked hard to ensure that departmental decisions were agreed rather than imposed, and that all staff were involved in planning schemes of work and identifying suitable resources. In the wider school setting, she acknowledged an accountability to the head, but did not believe any other line management arrangement had existed either before or after the restructuring. No one had ever come to her and commented on the quality of her management of the department, and she felt that as a head of department she had been given her area of responsibility by the senior management and left to get on with it. However, a new head was taking over at the beginning of the following term and that might change.

The main change which she faced as a co-ordinator was attending a newly created fortnightly meeting with the other seven co-ordinators and the curriculum director. The headteacher said that this had been set up because he understood that heads of department wished to take a wider part in the school's policy-making. The work of the co-ordinators' committee was formerly done by two faculty heads as members of the senior management team. Things were at an early stage when we spoke, and Christine was clearly finding the meetings difficult and frustrating. It was important, she said, for co-ordinators to remember that they were both representatives of their own area and members of a whole-school body which had to take a broader view of issues, and senior management would need to train the co-ordinators to take the wider view: everyone was tending to fight their own corner and put sectional interests first. In addition, much of the discussion seemed to be going nowhere, and it was important that the meetings should both sort out their own ground-rules and establish a clear role within the decision-making structure as a whole. This was difficult because, as another co-ordinator pointed out, the scheduling of the various school meetings made the 'upward' flow of information from departments to the co-ordinators' meeting easier than the 'downward' flow back. Consequently, although the publicly stated principle behind the new structure was that decisions should be taken at the 'lowest' possible position in the school, in practice it still looked as though the system was strongly centralised, with decisions being taken by senior staff on the basis of information flowing up through the hierarchy rather than by less senior staff on the basis of a two-way flow of information.

For Christine Urquhart, then, the problems she faced in her new role concerned her wider school responsibilities: her departmental duties were little different from those of heads of departments five years earlier, but the whole-school duties were entirely new. The headteacher saw the co-ordinators as the school's middle management: not all heads of department had this status. A similar forum had been created for the senior pastoral staff. They were to straddle sectional and whole-school interests, and resolve potential conflicts between sectional interests before the issue was discussed by senior staff. For Christine, this was something entirely new for which she and her colleagues were unprepared by their previous experience as heads of departments.

CONCLUDING COMMENTS ON THE SECONDARY CASE STUDIES

You will recall that the primary school postholders tended to be curriculum leaders, recognising an accountability to the head and acknowledging responsibility for planning, leading and advising, and to a lesser extent for monitoring, but not for direction and control. They wanted more integration of work, but struggled with a culture of integration. Somehow, they wanted to achieve a culture which simultaneously allowed integration and differentiation to occur. The language of co-ordination rather than management was more appropriate to those case studies.

In the secondary school cases this was less apparent. Three of the six heads of departments accepted the need to direct and control what was taught, and the other three acknowledged an accountability for what was taught. Both heads of science were comfortable with the ideas of planning and controlling what was taught, monitoring what was done and ensuring that syllabuses were followed. Their programmes of work were detailed, and they used the opportunities for practical work to regulate what was done through the provision of materials. The head of home economics accepted and relished the principles of command and control even as she denied them. All three saw policies and regulations as important parts of running a department, and were prepared to promulgate them. Their managerial style was bureaucratic if not autocratic, and they all sought to create strongly integrationist cultures.

The others were less comfortable with this directive managerial role. They sought to operate on a more collegial basis, having their departmental staffs agree on what was to be done and accept responsibility for delivery both individually and collectively, and then relying on the teachers to acknowledge the moral force of the 'contract' created by the free commitment resulting from participation. Consequently, they did not monitor practice in detail. Whereas the science and home economics departments were akin to machine bureaucracies or simple, power-culture systems, these were closest in form to Mintzberg's professionalised bureaucracy, being highly decentralised, allowing considerable latitude to the individual teacher, demanding less communication between them, and achieving the necessary co-ordination through the common skills and knowledge possessed by those at the core, so that the demands of the job were interpreted similarly.

A number of the factors we have discussed may contribute to these differences. The first is epistemological. Science and home economics are closer to objective, fact-based knowledge than English and history, and their individual teachers are more likely to accept direction from specialists. But where such consensus about content does not exist, as when Andrea Hackett took up her post as head of home economics, heads of department tend to fall back on coercion, as she did, or on a search for consensus through participation.

A second factor is departmental membership. The heads of history and maths, and one head of science, had highly experienced staff. How far they could exercise direction over others' actions depended on their sense of how far they had the expertise to ask others to conform to their requirements. The history teachers helped by asking for a statement of minimum expectations which reduced uncertainty and eased the preparation load for a group of very busy senior staff, whereas the equally senior and experienced science staff resisted any direction and had to be brought into line through less direct means – use of resources, through the good services of the laboratory technicians, and so on. This difference indicates that we cannot assume that more senior staff are at ease with the idea of direction and control because they are secure in their sense of professional competence, and welcome assistance in determining what their teaching duties are.

A third key factor is the sense of the head of department's individual competence and expertise relative to the others in the department. The head of home economics believed that she was both fully competent and right in her approach. She stated that she didn't have discipline problems, and only used the disciplinary system to keep the heads of year informed about developments or incidents that might be relevant to others' concerns or the personal well-being of a student. She therefore believed that she was fully entitled to lay down what should be taught, when and how. By comparison, the head of history doubted if he could give directions to much more experienced and well-prepared teachers than he, and the head of English believed that her experience was not sufficiently relevant to the new situation she faced in a comprehensive school to allow her to require anything of a department which was traditionally very independent if not fragmented.

A fourth, related factor is the concept of teaching underpinning the heads of departments' practice. Using the Wise *et al.* (1984) typology, the heads of history, maths and English clearly saw their colleagues as professionals and in need of administrative support rather than managerial direction, whereas the head of home economics viewed her colleagues as apprentices to craft status, needing tight direction and control. The heads of science appear to have viewed their staffs in two ways, depending on what they were teaching. They were professionals in their specialist area, but craftsmen and women when working outside it. Consequently, Euan Campbell found it hard to be directive except in his own specialist area, whereas it was easier for Henry Ashton, whose less experienced and changing staff needed to fit into a secure and established scheme for the sake of the pupils.

It may be that, in line with other studies of the role of teachers and what influences their approaches to their work (e.g. Sikes, Woods and Measor 1985, Siskin 1994), subjects are more important as a source of consistency than the school environment. Certainly the three departments at Sarah Lawley School were substantially different in culture, being respectively integrative and directive, integrative but collegial, and fragmented but increasingly integrated departments, However, we should not assume that because both heads of science saw themselves as entitled to exercise forms of control over their colleagues' work that their two departments had similar cultures, for one was far more integrated than the other, in which the prevailing norms were those of independence and non-collaboration. This would match Siskin's finding that there were different kinds of departmental subculture across subjects and schools, and the key variable was 'local environmental circumstance' – the people and the environment created by the head of department.

It is, therefore, also important to recognise the differences between how the heads of department view their wider context. It was common to find them protecting their department from the rest of the school, and those who recognised a wider responsibility than the narrowly sectional were struggling to come to terms with it, either because it was hard to break out of that sectional perspective or because the wider role they wished to play was not acknowledged by senior staff. Not one of the cases provided here demonstrated a department clearly at ease with the broader culture of the school and in harmony with it.

These case studies demonstrate a wide range of perceptions of the middle management role and proper behaviour within it. There is, perhaps, more consistency about the tasks they are concerned with than was suggested by the survey data, but their relative importance, and how they need to be carried out, clearly varies from setting to setting. Nor should any of these approaches be seen as ideal, or as examples of bad practice. The most appropriate way to handle a particular situation, and the most appropriate long-term management strategy, depends on the circumstances and the staff with whom one is working. The cases demonstrate how, although the technical 'skills' involved in activities like managing meetings and negotiating with colleagues are clearly important for successful and effective management, less immediately obvious responsibilities may be more important than the more technical matters if middle managers are to contribute to the smooth and effective running of their schools.

9

Improving Middle Management:
A Reflective Strategy for Personal Development

In this book I have argued that management in schools cannot be improved simply by taking a set of rules or tips and applying them, but needs to be examined in relation to a range of contextual factors. These include individuals' perceptions of teaching and schools, how the school is structured and operates, the culture of the school and units or departments within it, and the assumptions made about the basis on which it is appropriate and legitimate to attempt to influence other people's actions. In this final chapter, these points are summarised and a strategy outlined for you to use to analyse your own management development needs and to begin to address them. It is suggested that this involves moving from your personal values and assumptions through an analysis of the working environment, to relating these to the formal and informally stated expectations which are placed upon a particular role which you either hold or wish to obtain. It will then be possible to identify strengths and weaknesses in both the formal arrangements through which the work is carried out and in your personal abilities and skills, before considering how these individually diagnosed needs might be met.

SUMMARY AND REVIEW OF THE ARGUMENT

The idea of 'middle management' assumes a hierarchy of status in the organisation, with those in senior positions providing leadership and direction and those in middle ranking positions having responsibility for spreading understanding of the leadership and support for that direction so that everyone works to the same objectives. This is important in the light of the increased competition between schools in the government-created 'quasi-market'.

Management theory identifies four basic functions for which managers must take responsibility: 'production' or the 'core task' of the organisation; financial resources; people ('human resources'); and marketing the product. To do this, managers have to carry out a variety of duties. These include planning what is to be done within their area of responsibility, organising people and resources so that the plans can be carried out, commanding or giving instructions so that everyone involved is clear about their work, co-ordinating the work, including monitoring and evaluating process and outcomes, and controlling what is done. Some of these are more attractive to teachers than others. How they carry out these tasks varies depending on their personal values and those of the organisation, and on the circumstances in which they are operating. Managers can be seen to fulfil a variety of roles, which may relate to interpersonal, informational and decisional tasks within the broad responsibilities they have to discharge.

Individual and collective values are crucially important in shaping what is regarded as acceptable management practice. Organisations have cultures – patterns of norms and expectations – within which managers have to operate. In larger organisations, where there is more room for sub-units and departments to become established, these can develop subcultures which may be at odds with the prevailing culture of the whole organisation. 'Middle managers' have to operate in both cultures, and are pivotal figures in trying to bring both cultures into line – or choosing not to. In particular, the informational role they can play is crucial in this work.

Individuals bring together experience and personal values into an 'assumptive world' or 'theory in use' which guides them in defining a situation as one in which they need to take action and identifying what would be acceptable and appropriate action to take. Each assumptive world/theory in use is individual and largely unexamined until what it assumes to be 'right' action no longer appears to be dealing with 'problems'. They can be in line with the prevailing norms of colleagues and the formal statements of values promulgated at their place of work ('espoused theory') or substantially at odds with them.

A fundamental aspect of one's individual assumptive world as it affects one's management role is the concept of teaching which informs it. Teaching can be viewed as supervised labour, managed craft, administered profession, or encouraged art. Further, teachers may see themselves as subject specialists who teach, or as expert teachers who may have a specialist subject background. Specialists are concerned with imparting a body of knowledge and abilities, and are more likely to accept the principle of direction, which must be followed, whereas experts are more likely to deny it, but to acknowledge the value of advice, which can be accepted or declined.

Another important dimension of both personal and organisational values is the basis of one's right to influence another person's actions. Managers and others have access to different forms of 'power resources', which may include physical power to coerce, economic resources to use as rewards, knowledge which can be used or adapted, or 'normative' resources in the shape of ideologies or personal charisma which leads people to want approval for their actions. Authority is a form of power resource which is acknowledged as legitimate by those over whom it is exercised. Power resources are distributed through the organisation: those who are managed have resources too, because the manager depends on them for tasks to be completed. Compliance with the exercise of power resources may be willing or unwilling, and the more unwilling it is, the more the exercise of those power resources can alienate those on the receiving end and reduce the extent to which they are effective.

Ultimately, whether willing or unwilling, all compliance with the exercise of power resources rests on the basis of consent, but unwilling compliance is limited consent and may be withdrawn if those concerned feel that they have enough power resources at their own disposal to challenge those of the person seeking to coerce them. Compliance may rest on rational acceptance of the principles of the action required and its potential success, or on a pragmatic acknowledgement of the distribution of power resources at the time.

Consensus is not the same as consent. It implies that those who are involved in acting have freely and willingly agreed to the principles of action and will carry them out wholeheartedly. Consent may be pragmatically limited to an individual event or decision, and provisional in that it may be expected that an opportunity may arise to overturn the decision later, or undermine it because of the freedom of action – discretion – available to the people involved.

The principles upon which schools may be structured and operate may vary between the rational and the non-rational. How a school is organised and structured is important because organisations are created for particular purposes and how that organisation is put together influences the nature of the work which is done. The different principles on which the work of teaching children is structured is one fundamental reason why primary and secondary schools can be so different. Bureaucratic and collegial approaches to organising the management and operation of schools rest on the principle of consensus. In a bureaucracy, it is assumed that everyone accepts the assumptions which lead authority to be related to position, decisions to be centralised, jobs to be defined as they are, the relations created between the holders of different posts, and the principles of good practice upon which tasks are defined, outcomes assessed, and promotions awarded. Middle management has a responsibility to implement decisions faithfully and keep senior management informed of how they are working out in practice. Bureaucratic models are often assumed to be the natural form of organisation and the natural basis upon which management practice has to be built. Collegial models, especially popular in writing on primary school management, assume that all major decisions can be taken collectively, and the assignment of tasks and responsibilities can rest upon similar forms of consent. Middle management is a questionable concept in collegial organisations, since responsibility for implementing decisions is collective by virtue of the decision being taken democratically. These may be seen as 'ideal types' of organisational form, because in practice such consensus is difficult to maintain and the delegation of responsibility to the collective is problematic.

Political and subjective models rest upon individual rather than collective perceptions. Political models are rational, in that it is expected that each individual will calculate their own self-interest and act accordingly, creating and negotiating coalitions in order to pursue those interests. Decisions and their acceptance are therefore calculative, resting on limited consent rather than consensus, and the distribution of power resources will vary from instance to instance. Political activity can coexist happily with both bureaucratic and collegial organisational forms. Subjective models deny the existence of 'organisations' and 'organisational goals' except as collections of individuals and the goals of the most influential members, and see the management function as resting on how such individual stances can be worked out most effectively to create consistent work.

Ambiguity models treat all elements of the organisation of work as problematic: the goals are not clear, how they translate into practical activity is uncertain, and people only take part in decisions in so far as they are important to them at the time. Consequently, the relationship between problems and decisions on what to do about them – 'solutions' – is often unclear. In addition, the connection between different elements of an organisation is not always obvious, and parts may be able to operate largely in isolation from others. Middle managers in organisations which function on ambiguity principles have constantly to buffer their own units against unwise decisions and pursue sectional interests, while developing as much coherence within their area of responsibility as possible. Subcultures and differentiated organisational cultures are normal in such organisations.

Primary and secondary schools present different perspectives on the middle management role. Primary schools are smaller, and support a shorter career structure. More of the staff have to balance social expectations of domestic responsibility with their teaching career. Teaching is organised by age level rather than by subject specialism. Consequently, hierarchical structures and their associated delegation of responsibility, which encourage a bureaucratic ideal-type organisation, are less in evidence, and there is a greater expectation that individuals are directly accountable for their work to the head, rather than to someone else. This can encourage greater cultural coherence and integration unless the prevailing norms are those of autonomy and independence in a private classroom. Job descriptions emphasise creating guidelines, assisting and providing in-service training, while staff see themselves as having more responsibility for planning, organising and co-ordinating, and less for giving instructions and monitoring their execution. 'Middle management' is therefore a problematic concept in application to primary schools, although many staff have delegated management responsibilities.

Secondary schools are more inclined to be hierarchical and therefore tend to the bureaucratic, with stronger role cultures. However, the problematic nature of the 'technology of teaching' in relation to goals, allied to the different epistemologies behind specialist and expert teachers, can promote differentiated cultures which encourage micropolitical and ambiguity perspectives in their management. For specialist-oriented teaching departments, this strengthens the authority of individuals to direct and control others which is assumed in a bureaucracy, whereas in expert-oriented departments, there is a tension between the claim of professional autonomy and the responsibilities imposed upon heads of department or pastoral units by virtue of their office within a bureaucratic or hierarchical structure. 'Middle management' is therefore a productive concept in secondary schools, because it allows for the promotion of senior management's vision in the specialist sub-units and provides a vehicle for control and direction. It was difficult to pin down precisely who was regarded as middle management, and the case can be made for a distinction between staff holding three or four responsibility points, and who have a range of duties across the management spectrum, and those on lower salary positions who exercise fewer responsibilities and in smaller units. However, in practice, most people holding responsibility posts were designated 'middle management' by their headteachers.

There was some difference between individual interpretations of the head of department role, the duties which headteachers laid upon them in job descriptions and Ofsted expectations. Heads emphasised the creation of structures and guidelines and controlling and directing staff in their day-to-day implementation; Ofsted agreed, but also stressed medium-term development planning and a stronger evaluation focus which would be linked to that. There was clearly in both of these interpretations of the role a strong emphasis on integrating the individual teacher into a collective culture and centrally directed activity. Individual middle managers, however, interpreted the demands they faced by reference to their personal interpretation of the teaching role and the circumstances they encountered in their departments, and developed a far more fragmented response to basic responsibilities for organising the teaching of an area of the curriculum than documents and inspection reports might imply. The result was differentiated school cultures, with strong departmental subcultures and a tendency for political or ambiguity models to work for analytical purposes rather than the rational bureaucratic model of Ofsted and much management writing.

REFLECTIVE PRACTICE AS A BASIS FOR PROFESSIONAL DEVELOPMENT

The idea of the reflective practitioner (Schon 1983) has become a commonplace in much teacher education and professional development. It involves a deliberate attempt to analyse systematically the theories in use which inform individual practice, to identify the extent to which problems are created by the way their circumstances are interpreted in the light of those theories in use, and to develop new theories in use which can allow for new and imaginative solutions to be offered to problems. Theories of reflective practice rest upon views of adult learning, derived from the work of Kolb (e.g. 1984), in which a continuing cycle operates: a problem is experienced in some concrete form, which leads to careful collection of data about it and an analysis of those data. Thereafter, one attempts to re-formulate or 're-conceptualise' the problem in abstract, theoretical terms, in order to generate possible alternative strategies and actions to deal with it. The last phase is one of active experimentation to see if the ideas generated alleviate the difficulty. We then return to a concrete phase, which begins the next circuit of the cycle.

The starting-point of the process, therefore, is a concrete problem, and the intended outcome is some kind of changed activity which will resolve it. Along the way, knowledge is gathered and theoretical insights sought which will help you to rethink the problem. The process is well described by Osterman and Kottkamp (1994). A key element in this, often overlooked, is what Argyris and Schon (1978) christened 'double loop learning'. This is different from normal, 'single loop' learning because in normal learning situations we increase our store of information about a topic without questioning the underlying principles on which that knowledge is based. 'Double loop' learning, on the other hand, involves our deliberately and quite explicitly questioning the assumptions which lead us to define the problem in the way that we do. Thus, for example, we might face a difficulty with a particular group of children which all our normal teaching strategies fail to address. Single loop learning would leave us with a problem, because we would investigate and search for alternative teaching strategies which preserved our assumptions about what was proper teacher behaviour and pupil response. Double loop learning would enable us to ask if the problem lay not in the difficulty but in some aspect of the organisation of the school, or in the way in which we thought about our work or in the way we defined 'right' behaviour.

The content of this book has provided you with the means of undertaking a reflective approach to your personal development as a manager or prospective manager, by introducing you to a range of concepts and ideas about management, teaching and schools which may be helpful as you seek ways of analysing your data on problems and re-conceptualising issues. Writers in this field and practitioners of reflective practice-style consultancy sometimes appear to argue that because reflection on practice involves starting from immediate problems, such material must be ignored, but this is a mistake. Just because one starts from a practical problem or issue does not mean that we ignore 'theory': on the contrary, it is the potential which theory has to provide alternative ways of looking at a problem that permits the development of reflective practice.

A STRATEGY FOR PERSONAL MANAGEMENT DEVELOPMENT

The approach put forward here is necessarily presented as a general strategy, and to that extent derives from ideas of rational planning. Indeed, in places it suggests using some basic planning techniques. You may, therefore, find that you link your personal development planning to the institutional development planning you undertake at departmental, subject or whole-school level. But it is important to remember that reflective practice proposes a constant interchange between practical problems and ways of thinking about them – what Duignan (1989) calls a dialectic. You may find that instead of reflecting upon your abilities and circumstances as a manager, and regarding the question of your personal development as 'the problem' needing resolution, it is more helpful to start from concrete problems which need immediate attention, and use the process suggested here as a vehicle for developing an analysis and re-conceptualisation of the situation surrounding the immediate issue, rather than trying to develop a broader personal development plan. I would suggest, however, that moving towards a more reflective response to problems is in any case likely to generate a wider perspective on your personal development needs which will benefit from the sort of analytical approaches suggested here.

A five-stage approach to reflecting on your personal development needs is suggested, as follows:

- Analyse and scrutinise your personal values and expectations concerning teaching and your relationships with your teaching colleagues.
- Analyse and scrutinise 'external' factors to the school and sub-unit in which you work.
- Analyse and scrutinise the job description and others' expectations of the management role you hold.
- On the basis of the first three exercises, identify what elements of work are satisfactory, which can be systematised, and which need improvement or development.
- Identify how the improvements or developments might be achieved.

The rest of this chapter offers some suggestions for each of these stages. It indicates some sources of information available to provide data for analysis, and suggests some questions you might ask yourself – or other people. It also identifies some of the concepts discussed in the book which might prove useful as you think about the implications of what you have found. Neither the questions nor the concepts put forward should be seen as exhaustive! Indeed, they are merely starting-points for what can be a wide-ranging exploration of issues.

1. Personal values and expectations concerning teaching and teachers

This first stage asks you to put your own assumptive world and theories in use under the microscope. I suggest you take it in two parts. First, consider yourself. What view do you hold of yourself as a teacher: are you a labourer, a practitioner of craft skills, a professional, or an artist? What kind of advice, guidance, support or direction do you seek from others, and whom do you seek it from and why? Which teachers do you admire and respect most, and why? Do those you respect most hold the most senior positions in the school? If not, where do they fit in to the formal hierarchy of seniority? When, if at all, do you think it is acceptable to ignore instructions or directions? What degree of discretion do you think you should be allowed by others in carrying out your teaching responsibilities?

Second, consider the same set of questions in relation to those with whom you work, paying particular reference to two (or possibly three) groups: those staff with whom you work most closely, and those whom you most admire as teachers and as colleagues. If these groups do not include the most senior staff, consider the questions in relation to them too. What do you understand to be their own self-perceptions as teachers? Are these different at all from your own self-perception? In particular, are their expectations concerning discretion and freedom of action similar to or different from yours? These questions will give you some idea of the pattern of responses you can expect if you start to bring in changes in your management practice. They will provide basic information about subcultures within the organisation, and about the informal norms and values which underpin daily practice and interaction between colleagues.

How might this be done? Concerning yourself, there is nothing like some hard, quiet, reflective thinking! It is often easier to approach such questions, as the model of reflection outlined above suggests, by focusing on a concrete activity or event, and asking yourself, 'How did I act in that situation, and why? How do I feel I should have acted?' When you try to consider others, observation of how they act is obviously important: you can learn a lot about theories in use from the way they respond to situations. For example, if there is a fracas outside a classroom, do they walk on by or try and deal with it? If the latter, is their approach aggressive or apparently calculated to calm the situation down? How heavy-handed is the headteacher when he faces the year seven boy who has accidentally fired off the fire alarm? What do you make of the teacher who says to a year four child who shows him some good work he is proud of, 'you're not so stupid as you look'? In addition, you could do worse than ask them! Discussions on questions like those you have posed yourself can take place quite informally, and, once again, can often focus on specific incidents – 'here's an interesting problem, what do you think one ought to do?' is often a good starting-point.

2. 'External' factors

This is a very important stage. By 'external' factors I mean two things. First, there are the influences which the school has to respond to, and also the responses which are made formally to them. Second, the wider organisation is an external influence on the unit or sub-unit in which you work for most of your time and for which you are, or hope to become, responsible. Such organisational analysis is obviously essential for a newly appointed head of department, year or section as they take up post in a new school, but it is equally important for the long-established teacher: it is all too easy simply to carry on as we have always done. This stage of your analysis will therefore focus on the values and expectations of central government as communicated through policy statements, DfE/DEE circulars and Ofsted publications and reports; on the formal and informal culture of the school as a whole; and on subcultural factors.

When you are considering these questions, it is vitally important that you remember the distinction drawn between espoused theories and theories in use. This distinction is not limited to individuals: organisations or those responsible for the formal philosophy of the school and the official statements of individuals' responsibilities and obligations can achieve it too. Smith and Keith (1964) referred to the public statements of expectations as the school's 'façade'.

For this reason, although formal expectations can be established by a careful reading of official documents, it is not enough simply to read the documents at face value. Instead, you should tease out their underlying assumptions, looking carefully in particular at the language used. This is as true of government circulars and Ofsted reports and publications as it is of a school's formal policy statements. For example, Ofsted reports present a clear assumption that schools are rational organisations operating on rational management principles, with definable and measurable performance criteria. So you might ask if a document uses words like 'enabling', 'assisting', 'facilitating', 'promoting', or refers to people 'ensuring', 'issuing guidelines', 'following up', 'directing'? Does it talk about working together and collaborating with other individuals and departments, or emphasise individual accountability to unit leaders? Does it emphasise the personal development of the children or measurable performance outcomes? Each emphasis indicates a particular underlying philosophy, which may belie the apparent message of the document. This analysis will be able to draw on the discussion of organisational cultures and forms in Chapter 3 and, to a lesser extent, Chapter 4.

A key dimension of this second stage of the strategy, which arises out of examining underlying cultures, is a form of organisational analysis. In doing this, the discussion in Chapter 4 of different perspectives on organisational form and management practice, with its examination of power resources and the assumptions on which organisations are constructed and presumed to operate, is extremely productive. Much can also be learned about the informal culture of the school, and of sub-units within it, by observing how other staff act. If you are considering a post at another school, and are not given any opportunity to meet other staff in the department, or in the school, then you should consider why this happened. If you are beginning to review your understanding of your current place of work, then it is helpful to watch how staff act towards one another in the staffroom and at meetings. Who appears to dominate, and in what circumstances? Does it vary between settings and issues? For example, do some colleagues seem to be important figures in the staffroom but never speak in a formal meeting? It is also helpful to consider how meetings operate, what their purpose is, and how far formal intentions and areas of responsibility match with reality. Are they concerned with making decisions, making recommendations, or receiving information for their members to pass on? Is a working party really given freedom to explore the issue it has been set up to investigate, or are attempts made to influence its deliberations by senior staff or the head? Answers to such questions will help to generate information which you can analyse and re-conceptualise.

There are other questions you may choose to ask yourself about your colleagues. Are there particular groups who are visible in the staffroom, and others whom you never see there? (You may recall the history department in the secondary case studies which socialised with one another in the head of department's office, and was rarely seen in the staffroom.) Are there apparent barriers to contact between particular groups, and geographical 'zones' of the staffroom which have been colonised by particular groups? If so, are these groups based upon formal units or do they appear to be founded on some other basis? Are there separate staffrooms, for example on different sites? Do you feel comfortable in both? One split-site secondary school contained a clear group of staff who taught almost exclusively in the physically separate 'lower school'. It included teachers of history, art, science and languages, all of them women and most of them late entrants to teaching who had come through unconventional routes. It held together because they felt ostracised by their more traditionally qualified and largely male colleagues at the upper school and believed that they were discriminated against in the allocation of classes because however good their teaching might have been, they were seen as academically inadequate. Consequently, they ostracised in their turn, so far as they could, any upper school-based staff who came to the lower school.

Within your own immediate work environment, consider whom you feel able to talk to over professional and academic concerns, and which colleagues, if any, you tend to engage only in social chit-chat. Why do you tailor your contacts with your colleagues in the way that you do? Is there an element of your retreating from your staffroom into your classroom, and closing the door so that you can get on with teaching your class as you want to? Is that easy, or common, or widespread? What causes it? How important is your head of department or section leader, or the curriculum leader for that particular subject, as an influence on how you behave towards other colleagues and towards the children? Do you respond to school policies on pupil discipline by honouring them in the breach rather than the observance, and creating common cause with pupils to avoid trouble developing? It is not so unusual!

Questions like these can alert you to apparent inconsistencies between what people say and what they do, between the public façade and the practical reality, and between the formal structures and procedures and how they are used or evaded in practice. You have almost certainly asked yourself many of them already without formally articulating them: you develop images of how colleagues behave, and what it is appropriate to do with and for them, which influence your assumptive world and theories in use. I am suggesting that you make yourself conscious of your views of your colleagues and then explore their implications for your actions and theirs. Once again, the areas of the book which can help in this are those concerned with organisational form and culture and the cultures of teaching. In addition, the data you collect through this process of reflection and observation will shed considerable light on how you see power resources distributed within the school relative to particular issues, and how that distribution influences the operation of individuals and groups within the school's structure. Ideas of consent, consensus and compliance may also be fruitful, especially when you move on to the next stage, which will exploit your analysis of these first two stages.

3. The formal job description and others' expectations of the post you hold

With this third stage of the analysis, you turn from examining your assumptive world and theories in use about the context of your work to the work itself. In analysing the specific expectations laid upon you through the job description it carries, you will find it useful to consider your responsibilities from the perspectives of the management functions in which you have responsibilities, the management tasks you have to discharge, and the management roles you need to occupy in order to carry them out. This analysis and review can exploit the discussion of management in Chapter 3. It is a complex task, and we must spend some time considering it.

First, then, which management functions are you involved in – production (i.e. teaching and learning), resourcing, human resources (staff) or external relations? It is likely that all of them impinge on your responsibilities in some way. But they provoke different kinds of duties and obligations. The finance and resource function should, in a well-managed organisation, be coupled to the production function at the decision-making stage, but then the nature of the duties which follow, and what you have to ask of your colleagues, become quite different because of the presence of clear principles of financial accountability and practice. Which function is your primary concern? Further, are there any management functions which it would be helpful to have some responsibility for but which are not currently within your brief – for instance, are you a curriculum co-ordinator but without any budgetary responsibility? Alternatively, are there areas which you would like to pass on or delegate to someone else – would you rather move into a position which concentrated your responsibility in the financial area and removed your curriculum duties altogether? What would be the implications for your tasks and duties of any changes you would like to make?

For when you have identified the functional areas in which you have to operate, you must next identify which management tasks you are expected to do, and how these relate to what your functional responsibilities require. There are several categorisations to draw on for this in Chapter 3. All of them include, for example, the planning task, and some give some subdivision of this. Some of these tasks are likely to be acknowledged and accepted, but as the case study chapters revealed, others cause uncertainty and discomfort for postholders. In the light of the language of the job description, what others expect of you, and the formal and informal culture and structure of the organisation, you have to identify what tasks you need to be able to do and how far these match up with formal and informal expectations.

As an example, let us take the Adair (1983) categorisation laid out in Chapter 3. This identifies the following management responsibilities: defining the task, planning, briefing (i.e. ensuring that the team all know what they have to do), controlling, evaluating, motivating, organising and setting an example. I have chosen Adair because he distinguishes between your responsibilities for getting the task done, those related to the maintenance and development of the team you lead, and those for the individuals within the team, and recognises that the interests of each might be at odds with the others. He therefore stresses the interpersonal, leadership roles in management, and helps you to remember the assumptions you make about what people want and expect of you.

What, then, is involved in defining the task? Is it a 'given' that is handed down to you, or do you have the opportunity to participate in its definition? If you are responsible for a large department with other postholders less senior than yourself, then you may want to discuss the distribution of responsibilities with the headteacher who must finalise the job description, as well as with the individuals concerned. You may also wish to negotiate with senior staff the areas of activity involved in specific tasks – for example, if 'the task' is one of reviewing and amending the maths scheme of work, then you might wish to define the areas of responsibility relative to those of the teacher in charge of special needs provision, and in relation to budgetary responsibilities. Are you able to decide on and order resources for the replacement scheme?

The next task is planning. What activities have to be planned? What has to be included in the plans? What information do you require in order to be able to formulate your plans successfully? Whose co-operation do you require? Are there people whom you either wish or need to involve in the planning process, or depend on in some way if the task is to be completed satisfactorily? What tasks and responsibilities need to be allocated in order to execute the plan(s), and how can this be done? What do you need to know about in order to do this effectively? All these questions, which present an essentially rational perspective on the planning process, can help you to analyse what you have to do and give you pointers towards how it needs to be done.

One of the strongest elements of Ofsted comment in the early school reports was the focus on planning at the unit and sub-unit level. Heads of department were clearly expected to be engaged in creating medium-term development plans for their areas of responsibility, which would fit into the overall institutional development plan and provide a framework within which existing practice could be monitored and reviewed. In this way, Ofsted were looking for a detailed integration of financial, curriculum and human resource decisions – for example, a review showing that the department needed to develop a stronger focus on differentiation at the key stage 3 level, so that additional financial resources would be focused on providing greater variety of material and a member of staff would be identified to take responsibility for this, including receiving relevant in-service training and undertaking to feed her learning back to her colleagues.

The third element of Adair's approach is briefing. This is essentially about giving instructions so that all those involved in carrying out the plans know what is expected of them. It is easy to overlook this, especially if you have done your planning on a collaborative basis and assume that because everyone has contributed to the programme they all know and agree what they have to do. It is quite common for misunderstandings to develop which lead to key activities not being covered and things going seriously wrong as a result. However, you should think about how you go about such a briefing: do you simply give out tasks or instructions on the basis of what has been decided, or do you believe that you should allocate tasks collegially and then ensure that everyone has agreed on what they are doing? Here is a classic example of the way in which tensions can develop. You may feel yourself that your colleagues need to agree collectively to both the plan and the allocation of responsibilities, in order that they establish their 'ownership' of the programme. They may agree in principle, but be very busy and prefer to participate by making individual representations to you which you then weigh up before distributing duties. Individuals may prefer this as it gives an opportunity to complain about the allocation you have made, but not wish to accept the time commitment involved in the alternative. Briefing, then, involves important decisions on how you act towards your colleagues.

The next Adair task is controlling the work of others as they implement the plans in line with your briefing. This is often resisted. Do you need to 'control' what others do, or is 'monitoring' sufficient? What measures can and should you take to ensure that the agreed or established plans are being implemented? What forms of authority and expertise do you need in order to be able to take these measures? There may be forms of co-operation that you require, or information that you have to obtain. All of these need identifying, and with them the extent to which you are dependent on colleagues for them. The ideas of power resources and forms of compliance outlined in Chapter 4 are informative here.

I will only comment briefly on the remaining elements of the Adair list of tasks, for I hope that I have established some principles on which you can develop your analysis of your management tasks. The elements of evaluating and motivating are increasingly connected. Motivating staff is a complex responsibility when finances are tight and promotions increasingly difficult to come by, especially since many people joined teaching for reasons other than financial gain, and are now far more restricted in what they are allowed to teach than was the case even ten years ago. In addition, staff are now subject to appraisal, and although attempts have been made to separate appraisal activities from formal management responsibilities, it is impossible in practice to keep the two entirely apart. In a rational model of management, appraisal is a natural part of the process of monitoring and evaluating work, since it would link together a review of practice and achievement and a discussion of how one's colleagues can improve their performance and also achieve further professional development. Appraisal by one's 'line manager' would allow for the collaborative setting of individual targets for self-improvement in relation to an overall plan, and make it possible for the department to allocate or ask for resources to support professional development, as well as allowing for 'upward appraisal' (Diffey 1986) of the manager's performance and a discussion of how the manager could help in each individual's development. However, it implicitly asks managers to judge the performance of their colleagues, and that is problematic for many teachers because of their concept of autonomous professionalism. Evaluating and motivating one's colleagues, therefore, can present an acute difficulty for the educational middle manager, and along with planning shows how the reconciling of task, team and individual aspirations can be difficult. How you do this depends on how you resolve the tensions between your personal assumptive world and the organisation's culture and theories in use.

Organising the work within your area of responsibility is a basic task which is acknowledged whichever view of management, organisational form and culture and teaching underpins your view of your work. It is, however, closely related to issues of control, evaluation and motivation, since the more you feel you must define and control your colleagues' work, the more you have to organise the detail of schemes of work, resources available and access to them (will the video facility only be available for year nine for the first lesson of the week with each class?). Indeed, the detailed planning of access to facilities is often a crucial dimension of managing a department, since it is an important way of balancing individual and collective needs. The extent to which you see it necessary to do this collectively or as an executive responsibility which you exercise is an important aspect of your assumptive world influencing your approach to management.

The same is true of Adair's last management task: setting an example to your colleagues. Here he addresses the point that how one acts in a setting, and in relation to a particular issue, is more important than what you might say. In essence, it asks you to consider if you can do to and for others what you expect of them in return, and to think about ensuring that you demonstrate consistent and morally defensible actions as a manager of others.

The last element of this crucial stage of your personal development strategy is to consider the managerial roles you need to occupy in order to carry out the tasks you have analysed. In Chapter 3 we outlined the ten decisional, informational and interpersonal roles defined by Henry Mintzberg (1975/90). These are helpful as you consider in detail what activities you have to carry out in order to complete your management tasks. For example, when you are concerned with defining the 'control' responsibilities you have to exercise, you may anticipate being involved in decisional activities as negotiator, dealing with tensions that arise between individual teachers and between an individual teacher's wishes and the requirements of the course; as disturbance handler, when problems arise that you had not anticipated or resolved at an earlier stage, or when the materials for the new course, faithfully promised for September delivery by the publisher, haven't arrived; as resource allocator in terms of ensuring that all the classes have access to the books, equipment, videos and software when needed (and then as negotiator and disturbance handler when things go wrong!). In your informational roles, you will have been monitor as you ensure that things are going smoothly, and you may anticipate being a disseminator of successful practice you hear about (and perhaps of problems too) in order to promote a sense of collective progress through the year. You may also anticipate being a spokesperson to staff meetings and other fora which you attend, and these may lead you back into other decisional roles as you consider your relationship and that of your unit, to the wider school setting and other projects that may be in progress. And there will be important interpersonal roles: as leader of the department, you may feel obliged to 'lead from the front' in your teaching approach and taking on a fair share of the difficult classes, and in supporting colleagues when they encounter discipline problems. You may feel that you have an important figurehead role to adopt in relation to the rest of the school. And, as the informational and decisional roles have implied, you will have a major set of concerns to fulfil in your liaison role, where you are constantly checking on how things are going, identifying problems and opportunities, establishing individual needs and considering how they can be met.

The ten roles Mintzberg identified clearly interrelate, as the examples in the last paragraph show. You will also no doubt have noticed how 'control' issues tipped inexorably into matters of organisation, and it is important to remember that both are significant. Indeed, all these analytical approaches are concerned with creating handles on to which you can hang your ideas about what your job involves you in doing and what represents good and proper practice in carrying out your responsibilities. It is not intended to suggest that each is a discrete and separate responsibility that can be examined entirely in isolation. What is being suggested, however, is that it is possible to analyse a task in relation to the different aspects of work which need to be carried out for it to be completed successfully, so that strengths and weaknesses can be identified and exploited or worked on. A good example of such interrelationships being identified is to be found in Richards (1994).

4. What elements of your work are satisfactory, which can be systematised, and which need improvement or development

If you have established a clear picture of your expectations and those of your colleagues of what your management responsibilities are and how they should be performed, then you are ready to identify which elements of your work are being performed to your (and their) satisfaction, which ones could be dealt with without you having to be directly involved in action, and which ones need your action and can be improved. In this, a convenient approach is to modify what is called a 'SWOT' analysis, an approach often taken to management and policy development at an institutional level.

'SWOT' stands for Strengths, Weaknesses, Opportunities and Threats. It is sometimes presented in the reverse order, as 'TOWS', in order to emphasise that strengths and weaknesses relate to the circumstances in which they are being analysed. A strength in one setting might be a weakness in another, as in the case of the head of year who wished to operate her year team as a collegial, democratic unit but who was told by the head that this was wrong and that she was supposed to take decisions.

When you undertake a SWOT/TOWS analysis, you can exploit your thinking at previous stages of the review very effectively. You can distinguish between the management functions and tasks you have identified and the roles you occupy in performing them, and identify structural and interpersonal dimensions with their attendant value-bases and assumptions. You can also relate these findings and analyses to your individual assumptive world and its theories in use, in order to establish clearly where the strength or weakness you identify in your own abilities as a manager derive from a match or mismatch of fundamental values or from some particular ability or weakness of a more technical nature.

If we take the 'TOWS' approach, then the 'threats' you might face could include such interpersonal issues as uncertainty among the staff in your unit over your attitude towards them or to the direction in which the unit should develop, hostility on the part of individuals who were unsuccessful applicants for your job, or sexist or racist attitudes. Structural issues might include a conflict between your preferred approach to decision-making within your area of responsibility and that of the school's senior management, or finding that whole-school or cross-curricular fora are intensely micropolitical, which you have not had to cope with before. The two dimensions of structure and interpersonal issues might connect, for example if you identify one of your old-established unit colleagues who is clearly influential in an informal but very powerful alternative sub-unit within the staff, and who appears to have the ear of some of the senior management team.

Having identified threats and opportunities, it is appropriate to evaluate your own abilities in terms of strengths and weaknesses, bearing in mind that these relate to your circumstances. For example, you might feel that your success in bringing in some new teaching arrangements in your department although most of your colleagues were initially hostile shows that you are good at persuading people round to your way of thinking. This is likely to be a strength in any setting. On the other hand, your ability to organise arrangements efficiently and administer them well may be both a strength and a weakness if your colleagues feel that you should first of all gain their consent for the arrangements you make: that you should be their administrative agent rather than their manager. An ability to promote discussion, a willingness to listen to others' opinions and openness to suggestion may seem to you to be desirable qualities, but if your colleagues are used to a directive and hierarchical management approach, and consent to the centralisation it involves, then you have either to recognise your predisposition as a weakness or see the circumstances and your colleagues' attitudes as a threat.

A key dimension of this last phase is identifying specific skills that are strengths or weaknesses in the current setting, or that are likely to be important if you are trying to bring about changes in your area. It is convenient to group these skills under three headings. Some can be regarded as technical skills, such as basic book-keeping so that you can keep your unit's accounts straight. However, these will often be centralised for convenience and efficiency. Other technical skills are likely to relate to curriculum planning and evaluation, and are widely regarded as professional skills for all educators, not 'management' skills. Less likely to be so universally covered are the second category of interpersonal skills which are concerned with developing and sustaining a team within your unit. These skills relate in particular to the decisional roles of disturbance handler and negotiator and to the interpersonal roles of figurehead, leader and liaison. They may include approaches to dealing with and resolving conflict between colleagues and between others and yourself. Running meetings often figures in this area as a key set of skills needing development, and demonstrates how the skills you need are influenced by your intentions and beliefs in what counts as good management practice. If you believe that departmental meetings are for open debate leading to decisions, then you will want to develop a quite different dynamic within them from what would be appropriate if they were essentially for sharing opinions prior to your making the decision, and different again from what would be appropriate if you wanted to run a meeting as a means of passing on information.

Communication skills, which relate to your informational as well as your interpersonal roles, are also likely to figure in this area, both as strengths and weaknesses. You may, for example, feel that you need to improve your ability to interview colleagues, particularly if you are acquiring an appraisal role, or likely to have a part to play in selection interviews. Skills which will help you to put your interviewee at their ease, help them to make their expectations clear, ask questions which are open ended so that they give you expansive answers, support them when they find the questions difficult or threatening, cope with anger or other emotions when they show themselves, and draw the interview to a close so that your lines of communication remain open, might all be important interpersonal skills you decide need to be developed.

The third set of skills you may identify as strengths or weaknesses relate to your personal management of yourself. Two particular areas which often receive attention relate to managing one's own time and managing personal stress.

5. How to develop the skills you have identified as necessary

A number of courses of action are available to you. Long qualification-bearing courses involve a considerable commitment, but have the advantage of providing visible evidence of successful study. Increasingly they are focused on practical, school-based work and often involve forms of reflective action research. However, they are expensive and few schools are prepared to subsidise such personal development, often erecting a tension between 'institutional' and 'personal' development and denying the real benefits which such courses can provide for the school.

Shorter courses and in-house training sessions are more likely to obtain financial support, but the tension between individual and institutional needs remains an issue here too. Careful use of your own appraisal can help, as can identifying areas of responsibility or skills which several people feel need attention. An understanding of your school's decision-making processes and the distribution of power resources can be of great value here in influencing decisions on school-funded in-service training and staff development!

The content of in-house training programmes is, of course, negotiated between provider and clients. It is worth pointing out that this is also often possible, at least in part, for other shorter programmes, including those which are organised as small modules within longer, qualification-bearing programmes. This is not always realised by the participants, especially if they feel unsure about what they want or can expect. The kind of analysis advocated here, and which this book has sought to assist through the development of a management focus on the work of so-called middle managers, is invaluable in defining your own learning needs and therefore in influencing the content of your own professional development.

Alternatively, if all of these routes fail to deliver suitable training, you can always read books like this!

CONCLUDING COMMENTS

The middle management function in schools is likely to increase in importance over the next few years. The government policies which have delegated responsibilities for managing the education system to schools are not likely to be reversed by any change of national political control. Ofsted requirements are strengthening the expectation that schools will operate on rational planning and management models. Both make 'middle management' a function which is likely to develop, with all the possibilities of both strengthening and fragmenting the cohesion of individual schools. When you are promoted into posts which carry management duties and responsibilities, you will need to develop the technical, interpersonal and personal skills necessary to carry out those duties, but you will also need to become skilled at understanding and analysing the management implications of situations and developing ways of handling them which are in line with your own values and assumptions and those of your colleagues. Mere technical knowledge alone is not enough to make you a good manager.

This book, then, has attempted to analyse the context and assumptions in which you will be operating as a manager, and to provide you with a repertoire of analytical and conceptual tools to use in carrying out similar analyses of your own settings in order to identify your personal management development needs. There are plenty of opportunities around for developing the technical

and other skills needed, for 'middle management training' is a growth area, but the best way to make use of them is to relate them to concrete settings which you have analysed so that you can consider the problems involved as well as the technical opportunities for solving them.

Good luck!

Appendix:
Comments on the Activities

ACTIVITY 2.2

When I was a head of department myself I would have struggled to accept this idea. Indeed, I did not like the way that decisions were taken by the head through a bureaucratic consultation system rather than 'democratically' by a staff meeting or elected council. However, I had to acknowledge that the head (and the governors) approved my appointment as a head of department, and formally appointed me to carry out the tasks of running it. So however much I wished to claim a professional accountability to my departmental colleagues, I had to accept a formal accountability to the head for the way the department operated and what it achieved. I therefore had to accept that I could be instructed to operate in particular ways or do particular things.

ACTIVITY 3.2

I find much of this very helpful, even as I resist the idea of schools being rational, scientific establishments. Where it helps me is in terms of thinking about the work involved in middle management and the structures created for it. So the three ideas I would choose would be: the distinction between planning, organising, co-ordination, command, and control; the distinction between task, team and individual responsibilities; and the ideas of span of control and division of labour, which leads me to ask, why do we divide up our duties and responsibilities (including our teaching responsibilities) in the way that we do?

ACTIVITY 4.1.

One incident which left me with a strong sense of guilt occurred during my probationary year. I had difficulty with one mixed ability second year class, and with a small group of boys in particular. All of them were of low ability. I blamed all kinds of factors, in particular stressing that I was teaching history in a science laboratory, that the textbook was aged, and that group work was difficult because of the fixed benches and the nature of the materials. In the end, I complained about the class to the senior teacher, who told me to send out any children who were persistently naughty, since he was not teaching at that time and would deal with them. I finished up sending out one of the problem boys, and as I knew would happen, he was caned. I disapproved of corporal punishment but still followed the senior teacher's advice, knowing what he would do. Thus in my search for a 'quick fix' solution to an enduring problem I compromised my principles and allowed the school's normal approach to dealing with problems to operate.

It didn't work! At the next lesson, the class had decided to pay me back. No one spoke. All my efforts to get some question-and-answer activities going at the start were met with stony silence. This time I called in the head of house, but as she spoke to the class in front of me I realised that I was faced with a choice: to continue the strategy I had begun, or to reconsider my entire approach to teaching the class, recognising that the circumstances and the materials meant that everything I had tried to do for over a term was wrong. But to ask for help in an exercise like that in the early 1970s was risky. I decided to do so because I felt that having been baled out by senior staff twice in two lessons I would be running a greater risk by not doing it.

Thus this incident at the very beginning of my career faced me with a moral dilemma which I 'failed', in the sense that my desire for a solution to a problem led me to take actions of which I would have disapproved had I seen someone else do it. It was only when I was prepared to reflect on my assumptions about what was the proper way to teach my subject to such children that I was able to make any progress, and it took a lot to make me do this. Class and teacher made it to the end of the year without any further incidents of this sort, but it did not escape my attention twelve months later that barely one-quarter of this class opted for my subject, whereas in every other class the number was between half and two-thirds.

ACTIVITY 4.4

In a 'pure' bureaucracy, the decision would be taken by the senior staff. However, it would rest upon careful information having been passed up a ladder of offices, from individual teachers through their section leaders, and on to senior staff, if necessary passing through several 'rungs'. Along the way, individual section leaders would have investigated to see if the individual problem first brought to their attention was more widespread; if this had not happened, then senior management would have asked for it to be done, so as to make sure that it was not sufficient simply to issue a new regulation concerning the completion of the old report forms.

Once the decision was announced, it would be the responsibility of each section head to ensure that individual teachers completed it satisfactorily. However, to prevent differences of interpretation between the section heads, regulations would be framed and issued by senior staff which all teachers would adhere to. Difficulties in following the regulations would be passed up the line so that amendments could be made. All teachers would be happy to implement the regulations, since they acknowledged the goals of the change, and since it derived from senior management recognising an issue needing attention.

APPENDIX 4.5

In a collegial setting, the decision would have been taken in a full staff meeting. Prior to that, a problem or shortcoming in the existing report system would have been raised by a staff member in a staff meeting, which, if sufficient staff had acknowledged the difficulty, would have established a working party to investigate the problem and produce a recommendation for change. It is possible that there might have been a standing committee of some sort (perhaps on home–school communication) to which the issue would have been referred. Once a proposal was approved by the staff meeting, an administrator would take responsibility for ensuring that the report forms were ready, and individual teachers would take responsibility for using them in the way that was intended. The administrator might produce guidance notes for the completion of the new forms, but it is not clear that anyone would have the authority to enforce such procedures as they contained. Responsibility for collating the individual report forms would have to be allocated by the full staff meeting.

References

Adair, J. (1983) *Effective Leadership*, Aldershot: Gower.

Alexander, R. (1984) *Primary Teaching*, Eastbourne: Holt, Rinehart and Winston.

Alexander, R., Rose, J. and Woodhead, C. (1992) *Curriculum Organisation and Classroom Practice in Primary Schools: A Discussion Paper*, London: Department of Education and Science.

Argyris, C. and Schon, D. (1974) *Theory in Practice*, San Francisco: Jossey-Bass.

Argyris, C. and Schon, D. (1978) *Organizational Learning in Action: A Theory in Action Perspective*, Boston: Addison-Wesley.

Ball, S. J. and Bowe, R. (1992) Subject departments and the 'implementation' of National Curriculum policy: an overview of the issues, *Journal of Curriculum Studies*, Vol. 24, no. 2, pp. 97–115.

Beare, H., Caldwell, B. J. and Millikan, R. H. (1989) *Creating an Excellent School*, London: Routledge.

Becher, T. (1989) *Academic Tribes and Territories*, Milton Keynes: Open University Press.

Becher, T. and Kogan, M. (1980) *Process and Structure in Higher Education*, London: Heinemann.

Becker, H. S. (1962) The nature of a profession, in *Education for the Professions*, 61st yearbook of the National Society for the Study of Education.

Bell, A. and Sigsworth, A. (1990) Teacher isolation and school organisation in the small rural school, in G. Southworth and B. Lofthouse (eds.) *The Study of Primary Education, A Sourcebook, Vol. 3: School Organisation and Management*, Lewes: Falmer.

Bell, L. (1989) Ambiguity models and secondary schools: a case study, in T. Bush, (ed.) *Managing Education: Theory and Practice*. Milton Keynes: Open University Press.

Bell, L. (1992) *Managing Teams in Secondary Schools*, London: Routledge.

Bennett, N. (1981) Who takes curriculum decisions? Paper to ARMC/Schools Council Programme 1 Seminar. Mimeo.

Bennett, N. D. (1991) Continuity and change in school practice: a study of the influences affecting secondary school teachers' work and of the role of local and national policies within them. Unpublished Ph.D. thesis, Brunel University Department of Government.

Bennett, N. (1992) *Making Sense of Management*, Unit 1 of The Open University Course E629 *Managing Educational Change*, Milton Keynes: The Open University.

Bennis, W. G., Benne, K. D. and Chin, R. (1985) *The Planning of Change*, New York: Holt, Rinehart and Winston.

Bertalanffy, L. von (1973) *General Systems Theory: Foundations, Development, Applications*, Harmondsworth: Penguin.

Best, R., Jarvis, C. and Ribbins, P. (1981) *Perspectives on Pastoral Care*, London: Heinemann.

Best, R., Ribbins, P. and Jarvis, C. with Oddy, D. (1983) *Education and Care*, Oxford: Heinemann Educational.

Bobbitt, F. (1924) *How To Make a Curriculum*, Boston: Houghton Mifflin.

Bolam, R., McMahon, A., Pocklington, K. and Weindling, D. (1992) *Effective Management in Schools: A Report for the Department for Education via the School Management Task Force Professional Working Party*, London: HMSO.

Bottery, M. (1988) Educational management: an ethical critique, *Oxford Review of Education*, Vol. 14, no. 3.

Bottery, M. (1992) *The Ethics of Education Management*, London: Cassell.

Bottery, M. (1994) Education and the convergence of management codes, *Educational Studies*, Vol. 20, no. 3, pp. 329–43.

Boyatzis, R. E. (1982) *The Competent Manager: A Model for Effective Performance*, New York: Wiley.

Bryman, A. (1992) *Charisma and Leadership in Organisations*, London: Sage.

Bullock, A. (1988) *Meeting Teachers' Management Needs*, Soham: Peter Francis.

Burgoyne, J. (1993) Unpublished address to BEMAS Competency Workshop, Birmingham.

Bush, T. (1989) The nature of theory in educational management, in T. Bush (ed.) *Managing Education: Theory and Practice*, Milton Keynes: Open University Press.

Bush, T. (1990) *Theory and Practice in Educational Management*. Part 1 of The Open University Course E818, *Management in Education*, Milton Keynes: The Open University.

Bush, T. (1993) *Exploring Collegiality: Theory and Practice*. Unit 2 of The Open University Course E629 *Managing Educational Change*, Milton Keynes: The Open University.

Bush, T. (1995) *Theories of Educational Management* (2nd edn), London: Paul Chapman.

Campbell, R. J. (1985) *Developing the Primary School Curriculum*, London: Holt, Rinehart and Winston.

Campbell, R. J. and Neill, S. R. St. J. (1991) *The Workloads of Secondary School Teachers*, London: Assistant Masters and Mistresses Association.

Carr, W. (1987) What is an educational practice? *Journal of the Philosophy of Education*, Vol. 21, no. 2.

Cohen, M. D. and March, J. G. (1974) *Leadership and Ambiguity: The American College President*, New York: McGraw-Hill.

Cuthbert, R. E. and Latcham, J. (1979) Analysing managerial activities, *Coombe Lodge Information Bank*, no. 1410, Blagdon: The Staff College.

Day, C., Whitaker, P. and Johnston, D. (1990) *Managing Primary Schools in the 1990s: A Professional Development Approach*, London: Paul Chapman.

Deal, T. E. (1985) The symbolism of effective schools, *Elementary School Journal*, Vol. 85, no. 5, pp. 605–20.

Deal, T. and Kennedy, A. (1988) *Corporate Cultures*, Harmondsworth: Penguin.

Department for Education (1992) *Choice and Diversity in Education*, London: HMSO, Cm 2021.

Department of Education and Science (1978) *Primary Education in England: A Survey by HM Inspectors of Schools*, London: HMSO.

Department of Education and Science (1982) *Education 5–9: An Illustrative Survey by HMI*, London: HMSO.

Department of Education and Science (1987) *The Education (School Teachers' Pay and Conditions) Order*, London: HMSO.

Diffey, K. (1986) Upward appraisal, *School Organisation*, Vol. 6, no. 2, pp. 271–6.

Dobson, D. (1993) The Role and Development of Senior Management Teams in Secondary Comprehensive Schools. Unpublished BPhil dissertation, The Open University School of Education.

Donnelly, J. (1990) *Middle Managers in Schools and Colleges: A Handbook for Heads of Department*, London: Kogan Page.

Donnelly, J. (1994) People power, *Managing Schools Today*, Vol. 4, no. 3, pp. 16–17.

Donnelly, J. (1995) The mighty middle, *Managing Schools Today*, Vol. 4, no. 4, pp. 32–3.

Duignan, P. A. (1989) Reflective management: the key to quality leadership, in C. Riches and C. Morgan (eds.) *Human Resource Management in Education*, Milton Keynes: Open University Press.

Dunham, J. (1995) *Developing Effective School Management*, London: Routledge.

Earley, P. (1992) *The School Management Competences Project* (3 vols.) Crawley: School Management South.

Earley, P. and Fletcher-Campbell, F. (1989) *The Time to Manage: Department and Faculty Heads at Work*, Slough: NFER/Nelson.

Edwards, R. (1985) Departmental organization and management, in R. Edwards and D. Bennett, *Schools in Action. Welsh Office Research Project*, DES/Welsh Office.

Fayol, H. (1949) *General and Industrial Management*, London: Pitman (originally published in French in 1915).

Fielding, M. (1984) Asking different questions and pursuing different means: a critique of the new management training movement, in J. Maw (ed.) *Education plc? Headteachers and the New Training Initiative*, Bedford Way Papers no. 20, London: Heinemann.

Frohman, A. L. and Johnson, L. W. (1993) *The Middle Management Challenge: Moving from Crisis to Empowerment*, New York: McGraw-Hill.

Fullan, M. and Hargreaves, A. (1992) *What's Worth Fighting For in Your School?* Milton Keynes: Open University Press.

Fulop, L. (1991) Middle managers: victims or vanguards of the entrepreneurial movement? *Journal of Management Studies*, Vol. 28, no. 1, pp. 25–44.

Glatter, R. (1988) Introduction, in R. Glatter, M. Preedy, C. Riches and M. Masterton (eds.) *Understanding School Management*, Milton Keynes: Open University Press.

Glover, D. (1994) Ofsted and Middle Management. Research Report to Centre for Educational Policy and Management, The Open University. Mimeo.

Goodson (1983) *School Subjects and Curriculum Change*, Beckenham: Croom Helm.

Greenfield, T. and Ribbins, P. (eds.) (1993) *Greenfield on Educational Administration: Towards a Humane Science*, London: Routledge.

Gulick, L. and Urwick, L. (eds.) (1937) *Papers on the Science of Administration*, New York: Columbia University Press.

Hales, C. (1993) *Managing Through Organisation: The Management Process, Forms of Organisation, and the Work of Managers*, London: Routledge.

Handy, C. (1993) *Understanding Organisations* (4th edn), London: Penguin.

Hargreaves, A. (1992) Contrived collegiality: the micropolitics of teacher collaboration, in N. Bennett, M. Crawford and C. Riches (eds.) *Managing Change in Education: Individual and Organizational Perspectives*, London: Paul Chapman.

Hoyle, E. (1986) *The Politics of School Management*, London: Hodder and Stoughton.

Interim Advisory Committee (1990) *Third Report of the Interim Advisory Committee on School Teachers' Pay and Conditions,* London: HMSO, Cm 973.

Isabella. L. A. (1990) Evolving interpretations as a change unfolds: how managers construe key organizational events, *Academy of Management Journal,* Vol. 33, no. 1, pp. 7–41.

Jennings, A. (ed.) (1977) *Management and Headship in the Secondary School,* London: Ward Lock.

Keep, E. (1992) School in the marketplace? Some problems with private sector models, in G. Wallace (ed.) *Local Management of Schools: Research and Experience,* Clevedon: Multilingual Matters.

Kemp, R. and Nathan, M. (1989) *Middle Management in Schools: A Survival Guide,* Oxford: Blackwell.

Kolb, D. (1984) *Experiential Learning: Experience as the Source of Learning and Development,* Englewood Cliffs, N.J.: Prentice-Hall.

Kotter, J. P. (1977) Power, dependence and effective management, *Harvard Business Review,* Vol. 55, no. 4, pp. 125–36.

Lawrence, I. (1994) *Educational Management at Masters' Degree Level in English Universities.* A report to the Centre for Educational Policy and Management, The Open University School of Education, July.

Leat, D. (1993) *Managing Across Sectors,* London: City University Business School.

Lieberman, A. and Miller, L. (1984) *Teachers, Their World and Their Work,* Alexandria, VA: Association for Supervision and Curriculum Development.

Lipsky, M. (1980) *Street Level Bureaucracy: Dilemmas of the Individual in Public Services,* New York: Russell Sage Foundation.

Management Charter Initiative (MCI) (1991) *Management Standards Implementation Pack,* London: MCI.

Marland, M. (1981) Introduction: the tasks of a head of department, in M. Marland and S. Hill (eds.) *Departmental Management,* London: Heinemann.

Martin, J. and Meyerson, D. (1988) Organisational culture and the denial, channelling and acknowledgement of ambiguity, in L. R. Pondy, R. J. Boland and H. Thomas (eds.) *Managing Ambiguity and Change,* New York: John Wiley.

Mayo, E. (1933) *The Human Problems of an Industrial Civilisation,* Boston: Harvard Business School Division of Research.

McLaughlin, M. W. (1990) The Rand Change Agent Study revisited: macro perspectives and micro realities, *Educational Researcher,* December, pp. 11–16.

Metcalf, H. C. and Urwick, L. (eds.) (1942) *Dynamic Administration: The Collected Papers of Mary Parker Follett,* London: Management Publications Trust.

Meyerson, D.E. (1991) 'Normal' ambiguity? A glimpse of an occupational culture, in P. J. Frost, L. F. Moore, M. R. Louis, C. C. Lundberg and J. Martin (eds.) *Reframing Organizational Culture,* Newbury Park, CA: Sage.

Mintzberg, H. (1979) *The Structuring of Organizations: A Synthesis of the Research,* Englewood Cliffs, N.J.: Prentice-Hall.

Mintzberg, H. (1990) The manager's job: folklore and fact, *Harvard Business Review,* March–April, pp. 163–76 (originally published 1975).

Morris, J. (1975) Developing resourceful managers, in B. Taylor and G. L. Lippitt (eds.) *Management Development and Training Handbook,* New York: McGraw-Hill.

Nias, J. (1980) Leadership styles and job satisfaction in primary schools, in T. Bush, R. Glatter, J. Goodey and C. Riches (eds.) *Approaches to School Management,* London: Harper and Row.

Nias, J. (1992) Introduction, in C. Biott and J. Nias (eds.) *Working and Learning Together for Change,* Milton Keynes: Open University Press.

Nias, J., Southworth, G. and Yeomans, R. (1989) *Staff Relationships in the Primary School: A Study of Organizational Cultures,* London: Cassell.

Osterman, K. F. and Kottkamp, R. B (1994) Rethinking professional development, in N. Bennett, R. Glatter and R. Levačić (eds.) *Improving Educational Management Through Research and Consultancy,* London: Paul Chapman.

Rein, M. (1983) *From Policy to Practice,* London: Macmillan.

Ribbins, P. (1992) What professionalism means to teachers. Paper presented to the 1992 BEMAS Research Conference. Mimeo.

Richards, S. (1994) Curriculum Change in French, in M. Crawford, L. Kydd and S. Parker (eds.) *Educational Management in Action: a collection of case studies.* London: Paul Chapman.

Sackmann, S. A. (1992) Culture and subcultures: an analysis of organizational knowledge, *Administrative Science Quarterly,* Vol. 37, pp. 140–61.

Schein, E. J. (1983) *Organisational Culture: A Dynamic Model,* MIT/Sloan School of Management Working Paper no. 1412–83, Cambridge, MA: Massachusetts Institute of Technology.

Schon, D. (1983) *The Reflective Practitioner: How Professionals Think in Action,* London: Maurice Temple-Smith.

Shipman, M. (1990) *In Search of Learning,* Oxford: Blackwell.

Sikes, P. J., Woods, P. and Measor, L. (1985) *Teacher Careers,* Lewes: Falmer.

Simon, H. A. (1948) *Administrative Behavior: A Study of Decision-Making Processes in Administrative Organisation,* New York: Macmillan.

Siskin, L. S. (1994) *Realms of Knowledge: Academic Departments in Secondary Schools,* London: Falmer.

Smith, L. M. and Keith, P. M. (1964) *Anatomy of Educational Innovation: An Organizational Analysis of an Elementary School,* New York: Wiley.

Smylie, M. A. (1990) Teacher efficacy at work, in P. Reyes (ed.) *Teachers and Their Workplace: Commitment, Performance and Productivity,* Newbury Park, CA: Sage.

Tannenbaum, R. and Schmidt, W. H. (1973) How to choose a leadership pattern, *Harvard Business Review,* May/June, pp. 162–79.

Taylor, F. W. (1911) *The Principles of Scientific Management,* New York: Harper.

van der Vegt, R. and Knip, H. (1990) Implementing mandated change: the school as change contractor, *Curriculum Inquiry,* Vol. 20, no. 2, pp. 183–203.

Weick, K. (1976) Educational organizations as loosely-coupled systems, *Administrative Science Quarterly,* Vol. 21, no. 1, pp. 1–19.

Whittle, S. and Foster, M. (1989) Customer profiling: getting into your customer's shoes, *Management Decision,* Vol. 27, no. 6.

Winston, J. (1992) Reflective headship and ethical aspects of school leadership: a case study. Paper to the annual conference of CEDAR, April. Mimeo.

Wise, A. E., Darling-Hammond, L., McLaughlin, M. W. and Bernstein, H. T. (1984) *Teacher Evaluation: A Study of Effective Practices,* Santa Monica, CA: Rand.

Woodhead, C. (1995) *Education: The Elusive Engagement and the Continuing Frustration,* First Chief Inspector's Annual Lecture, London: Ofsted.

Young, K. (1981) Discretion as an implementation problem: a framework for interpretation, in M. Adler and S. Asquith (eds.) *Discretion and Welfare.* London: Heinemann.

Young, K. (1983) Introduction: beyond centralism, in K. Young (ed.) *National Interests and Local Government,* London: Heinemann.

Index